White bark pine on the rim of Crater Lake

50 *Hikes*

In Oregon

**Walks, Hikes & Backpacking Adventures
from the Pacific to the High Desert**

First Edition

DAVID L. ANDERSON

The Countryman Press
Woodstock, Vermont

AN INVITATION TO THE READER

Over time trails can be rerouted and signs and landmarks altered. If you find that changes have occurred on the routes described in this book, please let us know so that corrections may be made in future editions. The author and publisher also welcome other comments and suggestions. Address all correspondence to:

    Editor, 50 Hikes™ Series
    The Countryman Press
    P.O. Box 748
    Woodstock, VT 05091

LIBRARY OF CONGRESS CATALOGING-IN-PUBLICATION DATA

Data has been applied for.

ISBN 0-88150-652-4

Maps by Mapping Specialists Ltd., Madison, WI
Cover and interior design by Glenn Suokko
Composition by Doug Porter, Desktop Services and Publishing
Cover and interior photographs by the author

Copyright © 2005 by David L. Anderson

First Edition

Published by The Countryman Press
P.O. Box 748
Woodstock, Vermont 05091

Distributed by W. W. Norton & Company, Inc.
500 Fifth Avenue
New York, NY 10110

Printed in the United States of America

10 9 8 7 6 5 4 3 2 1

DEDICATION

To Oliver and Hayley, the two best hiking and camping partners any father could hope to have.

50 Hikes in Oregon at a Glance

HIKE	REGION
1. Saddle Mountain	Coast and Coast Range
2. Ecola State Park	Coast and Coast Range
3. Oswald West State Park	Coast and Coast Range
4. Cape Meares State Park	Coast and Coast Range
5. Munson Creek Falls	Coast and Coast Range
6. Cape Lookout	Coast and Coast Range
7. Drift Creek Falls	Coast and Coast Range
8. Cape Perpetua	Coast and Coast Range
9. Heceta Head	Coast and Coast Range
10. Kentucky Falls	Coast and Coast Range
11. Blacklock Point	Coast and Coast Range
12. Sauvie Island–Warrior Rock	Columbia River Gorge
13. Angels Rest	Columbia River Gorge
14. Triple Falls	Columbia River Gorge
15. Wahkeena Falls to Multnomah Falls	Columbia River Gorge
16. Wahclella Falls	Columbia River Gorge
17. Eagle Creek	Columbia River Gorge
18. Tom McCall Nature Preserve	Columbia River Gorge
19. Lost Lake	Cascade Range
20. Cooper Spur	Cascade Range
21. Elk Meadows/Gnarl Ridge	Cascade Range
22. Tamanawas Falls	Cascade Range
23. Ramona Falls	Cascade Range
24. Silver Falls	Cascade Range
25. Opal Creek	Cascade Range

DISTANCE (miles)	VERTICAL RISE (feet)	VIEWS	WATERFALLS	CHILDREN	DIFFICULTY	HIGHLIGHTS
5½	1,620	★			D	sweeping views, wildflowers, geology
6½	800	★		★	M	ocean views, beaches
7	300	★		★	M	ocean views, beaches
3½	600	★		★	M	ocean views
¾	100		★	★	E	waterfall
4¾	400	★		★	E	ocean views
3	350		★	★	E	waterfall
4¾	400	★		★	E	ocean views, beaches
4½	600	★		★	M	ocean views, beaches
4¼	750		★	★	M	waterfall
6¾	200	★	★		M	ocean views, geology
7	0	★		★	E	river views, wildlife
4½	1,400	★	★	★	M	gorge views
4½	700		★	★	M	waterfall
2¾, 5¼	1,200, 2,300		★		M	waterfalls
1¾	300		★	★	E	waterfall
12½	1,200		★		D	waterfalls, geology
5½	1,400	★		★	M	gorge views, wildflowers, geology
3¼	100		★	★	E	mountain views, lake
7¾	2,800	★			D	sweeping views
6¾, 10¼	1,200, 2,200	★			D	sweeping views, wildflowers
3¾, 5¾	500, 850		★	★	M	waterfall
7	1,000		★	★	M	waterfall
7½	600		★	★	E	waterfalls
7	400		★	★	E	waterfall, old-growth forest

50 Hikes in Oregon at a Glance

HIKE	REGION
26. Sahalie Falls	Cascade Range
27. Proxy Falls	Cascade Range
28. Tam McArthur Rim	Cascade Range
29. South Sister	Cascade Range
30. Salt Creek Falls	Cascade Range
31. Metolius River	Cascade Range
32. Susan Creek Falls	Cascade Range
33. Twin Lakes	Cascade Range
34. Toketee Falls	Cascade Range
35. Mount Thielsen	Cascade Range
36. Crater Lake	Cascade Range
37. Mount Howard Summit Loop	High Desert
38. BC Creek Falls	High Desert
39. Eagle Cap	High Desert
40. Hurricane Creek/Echo Lake	High Desert
41. Eureka Point	High Desert
42. Leslie Gulch	High Desert
43. Jordan Craters	High Desert
44. Oregon Trail Interpretive Center	High Desert
45. John Day Fossil Beds	High Desert
46. Smith Rock	High Desert
47. Fort Rock	High Desert
48. Newberry Volcano	High Desert
49. Big Indian Gorge	High Desert
50. Pike Creek	High Desert

DISTANCE (miles)	VERTICAL RISE (feet)	VIEWS	WATERFALLS	CHILDREN	DIFFICULTY	HIGHLIGHTS
1½	200		★	★	E	waterfalls
1½	200		★	★	E	waterfalls
7¼	1,600	★			M	sweeping views, geology
12	4,900	★			VD	sweeping views, summit hike, geology
3½	400		★	★	E	waterfall
5½	100		★	★	E	river springs, geology
2¼	300		★	★	E	waterfall
3¼	400	★		★	E	lakeside family backpacking
¾	100		★	★	E	waterfall
10	3,800	★			D	sweeping views, summit hike, geology
1–5	100–1,400	★	★	★	E-M	sweeping views, Crater Lake, geology
5½	1,100	★		★	M	sweeping views, tram ride
2¾	400		★	★	E	waterfall
14¾, 19¾	2,000, 4,000	★	★		D-VD	sweeping views, Eagle Creek, summit hike
10, 15½	1,000, 3,400	★	★		M-D	sweeping views, Hurricane Creek, alpine lake
7¼	1,800	★		★	M	sweeping canyon views, geology
3½	600	★		★	E	canyon views, geology
1	150	★		★	E	geology
3	350	★		★	E	history
3	400	★		★	E	views, geology
6, 4	200, 700	★		★	E-M	canyon views, geology
1¾	200	★		★	E	geology
¾–8½	200–500	★	★	★	E-M	views, geology
12½	1,300	★		★	D	canyon views, geology
2¾	850	★		★	E	desert views, geology

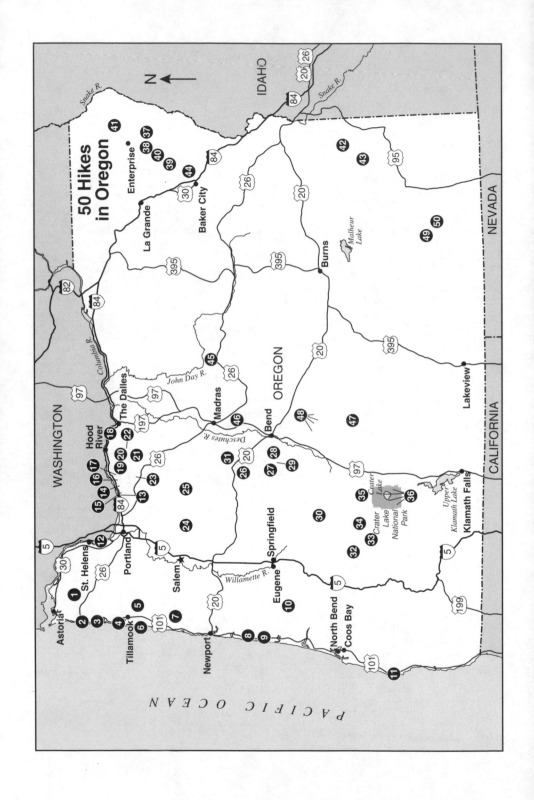

CONTENTS

IV. High Desert / 169

Acknowledgments

I would first like to thank all those people I've met along the trails and in the towns throughout the state for their kindness, generosity, and local wisdom. Thanks also to my parents, Louie and Linda Anderson, and to Stefanie Gunderson for her encouragement and review of the first drafts.

I would also like to thank Richard Fumosa for his knowledge, patience, and guidance in editing this book. I would also like to extend my appreciation to Kermit Hummel, Jess Abston, Ann Kraybill, Bill Bowers, and the staff at The Countryman Press for all their help.

Introduction

In a state that cherishes and utilizes its wilderness as much as Oregon, selecting only 50 hikes is a challenge. It also means that some, in fact a great many, will be left out. In choosing the hikes in this book, I selected those that best represent the state, the region, and its natural wonders. The hikes have also been grouped so that several hikes can be performed in a weekend. The hikes vary in length, elevation, and difficulty in order to appeal to a wide range of abilities. This collection of hikes also represents some of my personal favorites.

OREGON

Driven by countless reasons, free land, riches, fleeing persecution or economic strife, or just a sense of adventure—nearly 500,000 Americans left their former life behind and headed west along the Oregon Trail. What they found was a land of fertile valleys, towering peaks, endless forests, and, at the end of the journey, the Pacific Ocean. On February 14, 1859, these same pioneers celebrated the entry of Oregon as the 33rd state to a still youthful nation.

Oregon's 96,000 square miles makes it the 10th largest state in the United States. The state is bordered to the north by Washington, with Idaho to the east, Nevada and California to the south, and the Pacific Ocean to the west. There are 40 federally designated wilderness areas, about 3½ percent of the state's land. More than 70 percent of the 3½ million residents live in or around the Willamette Valley cities of Port-

land, Salem, Corvallis, and Eugene. In stark contrast, the southeastern portion of the state has a population density similar to Alaska. (At times this population disparity has generated some mistrust between the generally liberal metro regions and the predominantly conservative rural regions.)

Oregon's rainy reputation most likely originated from visitors to the Willamette Valley during the winter months or from the millions of tourists who visit the coast each year. Along the headlands and in the Coast Range annual precipitation may reach more than 100 inches. However, east of the Cascades the annual precipitation drops below 30 inches per year with several towns boasting more than 300 days of sunshine annually.

Although extremes do occur, the climate is generally moderate. Average summer temperatures along the coast are in the 60s and 70s, and in the 50s during the winter. Temperatures in the valleys typically average 5 to 10 degrees warmer. The greatest temperature variations occur east of the Cascades where summer temperatures can go from near freezing at night to the upper 80s or 90s in the afternoon.

GEOLOGY

In the context of geological time Oregon is relatively young. Approximately 400 to 300 million years ago the Pacific shore was situated just off the present border between Idaho and Oregon, and just offshore were a series of islands—the only landmass at that time of the present state of Oregon. As the

North American landmass, or plate, drifted westward over the Pacific Plate, the islands were lifted. Evidence of this process can be seen by examining the fossil remains of the Hell's Canyon area. This same process continues today. Geologic measurements of Cape Blanco indicate that it is rising at a rate of almost 3 inches per 100 years, among the fastest of any landmass in the world.

Between 20 and 15 million years ago, several massive fissures in the earth's crust opened, causing a series of basalt lava eruptions known as the Columbia River Basalt Lava Flows. They traveled as far as 300 miles, reaching the Pacific, extending the coastline and creating many headlands we see today, such as Cape Lookout, Tillamook head, and Cape Meares.

The first recognizable peaks of the Cascades began to form a little more than 1 million years ago. Beneath what are now the Cascades, a dense, oceanic plate began to plunge beneath the North American Plate. As this process occurred, high temperatures and pressures allowed water molecules to escape. The hot vapor caused the pliable mantle to melt, and the newly formed magma rose toward the surface to erupt, forming the chain of volcanoes. Many of these volcanic peaks fell dormant and were heavily eroded by a succession of glaciations such as Mount Washington and Three Fingered Jack. Others, such as Mount Hood and South Sister remained active and resisted the erosion of the glaciers. Both mountains are still active today.

During the last Ice Age, ending about 10,000 years ago, one of the world's most catastrophic geologic events helped carve the Columbia River Gorge. Near the city of Missoula, Montana, an immense lake formed behind an ice dam. The water levels rose, ultimately broaching the dam, sending one of the planet's largest floods across the eastern Washington landscape. The floodwaters carved the potholes of the Palouse and the Washington Coulees, creating an inland freshwater sea out of the Willamette Valley. As the ice and rock-laden floodwaters reached the Columbia River Gorge, they scoured it clean, leaving the hanging valleys that form the waterfalls we see in the gorge today. Remarkably, geologic evidence suggests that this scenario may have been repeated as may as a hundred times.

COMMON PLANTS AND TREES OF OREGON

Named for the early Northwest explorer and botanist David Douglas, the strong and lightweight lumber from the Douglas fir *(Pseudotsuga menziesii)* has been the lifeblood of the Pacific Northwest timber industry. As one of the most important timber species, the Douglas fir ranks first in the world as a source of lumber and veneer. In the past, it served as an important source for spear handles, harpoon shafts, dip-net poles, and fishing hooks for early Native Americans. The Douglas fir also ranks as one of the world's largest trees, with mature growth easily reaching 300 feet in height. Thriving in both wet and dry environments, its range extends from central British Columbia south to central California and east from the Pacific Coast over the Cascades with large stands in the Blue and Wallowa Mountains. Large forests of these Douglas firs can also be found throughout the Rockies. Older specimens are distinguished by their thick and deeply furrowed, reddish-brown bark. The flat, yellowish-green needles are approximately ¾ to 1 inch in length and have one groove on top and two white bands of stomata (tiny openings in the plant's skin) on the bottom. ·

Perhaps the second most common tree species in the Pacific Northwest is the western hemlock *(Tsuga heterophylla);* its range is similar to that of the Douglas fir, although the western hemlock extends farther north into southern Alaska. Mature trees may reach a height of 200 feet and can be identified by short, flat needles that are yellowish-green on top and whitish-green on the bottom. Its thick, reddish-brown bark is deeply furrowed in older trees and has a scaly appearance. However, one of the most telltale signs of the hemlock is its droopy top. Native peoples used the high tannin content in the bark to tan hide and to color baskets, using the wood to fashion spoons, roasting spits, combs, spear shafts, and children's bows. Today, hemlock is an important pulpwood and a source of alpha cellulose, which is used in making cellophane, rayon yarn, and plastics.

Western red cedar *(Thuja plicata)* is one of the most recognizable conifers in the western forest. Mature trees often reach a height of 180 feet with a wide base that is often fluted or buttressed. Its stringy, reddish-brown bark and flat, glossy, yellowish-green needles, which appear segmented or scalelike, give it a very distinct appearance. Western red cedars can be found in moist or wet areas along streams and lakes, and its range extends from northern California to the southwest portion of Alaska and east from the coast to the Cascades.

Native peoples greatly valued the cedar and used the easily split and rot-resistant wood for dugout canoes, posts, and totem poles. The bark was used for such items as clothing, blankets, baskets, and hats.

Native peoples believed the cedar had great spiritual and healing properties, and it has been said that one could gain strength by just standing next to the tree.

Sitka spruce *(Picea sitchensis)* is the world's largest spruce; mature trees reach a height of more than 160 feet. Its 1-inch-long, bluish-green needles are stiff and very sharp and were believed by Native peoples to have special protective powers. Its range extends along a very narrow belt in the fog zone along the Pacific Coast, from northern California to southern Alaska. Sitka spruce produce a high-grade lumber, and it is the main timber tree in Alaska.

The neat and tidy ponderosa pine *(Pinus ponderosa)* can be found primarily on the east side of the Cascades and range from southern British Columbia south to lower California and eastern Utah, New Mexico, Arizona, Colorado, Idaho, Montana, and Wyoming, where it thrives on the slopes of the Cascade and Rocky Mountains. Ponderosa pines commonly reach a height of more than 130 feet; it can be identified by its thick, furrowed reddish-brown bark, which is arranged in large irregular plates. Its stiff, dark green needles range in length from 4 to 8 inches. Its heavy and durable wood makes it the most commercially important pine in the West.

An irregular shape and twisted trunk are the distinguishing features of the subalpine white bark pine *(Pinus monticola).* Its needles are a dull, dark green and about 5 inches in length, with very fine white lines on the top and bottom. Rarely reaching a height of more than 50 feet, it's at home on the dry, rocky soil near timberline, ranging along the crest of the Cascades and Rockies from northern California and central Idaho to central British Columbia. White

Sitka spruce

bark pine is considered to be one of the most primitive of the native pines found in the Pacific Northwest.

Lodgepole pine *(Pinus contorta)* minimizes its competition by thriving in the poorest of soils. It can be found in higher altitudes and ranges from Alaska, northern British Columbia, and Alberta to southern California and New Mexico. These tall, narrow trees reach heights of 80 feet and have a thin, scaly, light-brown bark. The needles grow in bundles of two, which vary in color from yellow-green to dark green. Its name was derived from a Native American practice of using the slender trunks in the construction of teepees and tents.

One of the most common trees in eastern Oregon is the western juniper *(Juniperus communis)*. Although ragged and gnarled juniper trees rarely reach a height greater than 30 feet, they are among the oldest on the planet, reaching ages of more than 2,000 years. Its gray-green needles, mixed with whitish-blue berries, are short (¼ to ½ inch in length), stiff, and very sharp. Its range extends from eastern Washington south to southern California along mountain slopes and plateaus and in shallow rocky soil.

The Pacific rhododendron *(Rhododendron acrophyllum)* is one of the signature plants of the Pacific Northwest. Its pink and rose-colored blooms in the early spring add a splash of color to the green conifer forests. The range of the rhododendron extends from northern California north to southern British Columbia and east from the coastline to the crest of the Cascades. Thriving in the dry, acidic soil of conifer forests, it can reach a height of 20 feet. The leaves of this woody shrub are dark green, thick, and leathery, and its

flowers grow in bunches and are bell-shaped with wavy edges.

Among the most common understory plants in the coastal forest is salal *(Gaultheria shallon)*. Varying greatly in height, from 1 foot to more than 15 feet, the plant grows in dense layers. Its shiny, dark-green leaves are thick and leathery. In early spring its flowers are white and lantern-shaped, and the dark purple berries it produces were once an important food source for Native peoples. Salal's range extends along the coast west of the Cascades from northern California to southern Alaska.

The gray-green woody sagebrush covers much of eastern Oregon, and can be identified by its distinctive sage aroma. Its range extends from southern British Columbia south to southern California and east to North Dakota, Arizona, and New Mexico. In the deep, fine soils of the arid basins, it grows to a height ranging from 2 to 15 feet.

Oregon grape *(Mahonia nervosa)* is the state flower, and can be easily identified by its hollylike leaves and clusters of blue-colored berries that are edible but quite sour. Its small, bright yellow flowers grow in clusters and are in bloom from May to June. Native peoples have used the bright yellow inner bark as a dye for baskets and a combination of the berries and bark as a medication for eye problems. It can be found at low to moderate elevations, in dry to moist soils, and in open to closed forest areas. Its range extends from British Columbia south to central California and east to Alberta, Montana, Colorado, and western Texas.

Vine maple *(Acer circinatum)*, which grows as a shrub or small scraggly tree, commonly reaches a height of 20 feet. Its

Oregon grape

broad, 2- to 5-inch-wide leaves have a classic maple shape with seven to nine points. In the fall the leaves turn golden yellow to bright red adding a splash of color to the forest understory. It can be found in moist or wet areas in the underbrush near openings in the canopy and ranges west of the Cascades. The dense, hard wood was used by Native peoples for snowshoe frames and drum hoops.

Commonly found in the low, swampy areas of the Coast Range and western Cascades, skunk cabbage or swamp lantern *(Lysichiton americanum)* is easily recognized by its large, broad leaves and distinctive greenish-yellow spike and the bright yellow hood of its single early spring bloom. Native peoples used the large leaves as a lining for baskets and steaming pits. Although rarely eaten in a normal year, it was an important food source during times of hardship or famine.

The common red paintbrush *(Castilleja miniata)* is one of the most common wildflowers in the west. It can be found in open woods, meadows, grassy slopes, coastal marshes, and gravel bars, and ranges from sea level to subalpine regions. Its tall purplish stems rise between 1 and 3 feet above a woody base. Along the stem, narrow and sharply pointed green leaves alternate to the bright red tubular flower at the top, which blooms from May to September. Paintbrush is a partial parasite, wrapping its roots around those of nearby plants and using them to help gather water and nutrients from the soil.

Lupine *(Lupinus polyphyllus)* is one of the largest and showiest wildflowers in the state with its blue- to violet-flowered stalks reaching 5 feet in height. Its range extends from British Columbia to the costal ranges of central California and east to Alberta, Montana, and Colorado. It can be found in open areas with damp or wet soil; the taller large-leaved variety can be found from sea level along the Pacific coastline to the middle elevations of the Coast Range and Cascade foothills.

The smaller Arctic variety of lupine *(Lupinus arcticus)* can be found from the middle elevations of the Cascades and eastern deserts to the subalpine regions of the Cascades and Wallows. Long stems branch off the thick, green central stock and end at a starburst of five to 15 thin, narrow, green leaves. Atop the main stock is a large, elongated cluster of pealike blue or violet flowers that can extend up to 2 feet and bloom from May to September.

Several varieties of penstemon are common throughout the state. The flowers of the penstemon are tubular with ruffled edges and bloom from May to August. The coastal penstemon *(Penstemon serrulatus)* has broad oblong leaves, with its dark blue to light purple flowers growing in a cluster at the end of a short stem. It can be found along streambeds and on moist rocky slopes from sea level to the subalpine region of the western Cascades. Davidson's penstemon *(Penstemon davidsonii)* has individual purple or lavender flowers and creeps along the ground on the rocky slopes of the subalpine regions in the Cascades, Wallows, and Steens Mountains. The blue to purple flowers of the small-flowered penstemon *(Penstemon procerus)* cluster around a central stock. It populates the dry, sandy soils of the high desert.

Predominant on the east side of the state, the sunflower-like balsam root *(Balsamorhiza sagittata)* can be found on open hillsides, grasslands, sagebrush, and open pine forests. Its single, bright yellow flower grows atop a single nearly leafless stalk and can reach a height of 3 feet. It typically blooms from May to August.

The cloverlike oxalis *(Oxalis oregano)*, also known as redwood sorrel, grows throughout the Coast Range and on the west side of the Cascades. It grows at lower elevations in moist, forested areas often near streams. Its tiny flowers, ¼ to ½ inch in diameter, range in color from white to a pale pink with reddish veins decorating the plant's green, often carpet-like, growth. To conserve moisture the leaves fold in half in direct sunlight and during the night.

The beautiful bluish-purple color of the Oregon iris *(Iris tenax)* can be found in open grassy meadows, along trails, and in open woodlands at low to medium elevations on the west side of the Cascades. A single flower, ranging in color from purple to lavender and highlighted by white and yellow, tops a thin stem, which often reaches a height of more than 2 feet. The long thin leaves are very tough, and Native peoples often braided them into snares for animals as large as elk.

The distinctive, bird-bill-like flowers of the shootingstar *(Dodecatheon pulchellum)* can be found in moist meadows, among coastal rocks, and along stream banks throughout the state, but most predominantly on the west side of the Cascades. Although most common at lower elevations, it can be found in the alpine region as well. Its spring to midsummer flowers are ½ to 1 inch in length, with long, swept-back magenta petals. Two to three flowers sit atop each reddish stem, which may reach a height of approximately 1 foot.

Common foxglove *(Digitalis purpurea)* is a large and very showy flower that blooms in midspring and lasts throughout the summer. It is found on the west side of the Cascades at low elevations near trails, roadsides, forest edges, and in open fields. Its large, tubular, pinkish-purple flowers surround a single stalk, which may reach 6 feet in height. It was introduced to the Northwest from Europe, and it contains cardiac glycosides, substances that are highly poisonous. Despite this, the heart drug digitalis is derived from the plant's toxin and is used by thousands of patients suffering from heart disease.

Western trillium (Trillium ovatum) is common in the shaded open areas of the forests west of the Cascades and near stream banks. Its white, triangular, three-petaled flowers are easily recognized. It blooms early in spring when robins first appear, or "wake," which explains its common name, wake-robin.

PHOTOGRAPHY

The diversity that provides the state with so many hiking options also offers the photographer an endless abundance of subjects. From the ever-changing faces of the Pacific to the towering peaks of the Cascades, to the stark beauty of the eastern desert, the Oregon landscape offers a wealth of photographic opportunities. This same diversity also provides some unique photographic challenges. On any given day you can be deep in the shade of an old-growth forest in the morning and the barren sagebrush desert in the afternoon.

The lighting conditions for each of these regions may be drastically different, thereby requiring different methods to achieve the desired results. Regardless of whether you are using a digital camera or one that uses film, in order to create a good image, you have to achieve the correct exposure, which involves knowing how to allow the correct amount of light to hit the film or chip. If you overexpose the image it looks washed out and the colors will appear pale and too light. Underexposing the image will result in one that is dark and lacking in detail.

Exposure, aperture, and shutter speed

In theory, an exposure is correct if it is true to what the eye sees. In practice, however, there is no simple definition of correct exposure. Some photographers prefer images that are a bit darker, while some people consider an image well exposed if they can see the subject and make out the surroundings. Obtaining the correct exposure is a balancing act between the shutter speed of the camera and the aperture of the lens.

The lens aperture is a small, shutter-like opening that controls the amount of light that enters the camera. The speed at which the shutter opens and closes controls how long the film or chip is exposed to incoming light. The lens aperture size and the shutter speed work together to control exposure. When the lens aperture is small, less light enters the camera and a longer shutter speed (also known as a 'slow' shutter speed) will be needed to achieve a balanced exposure. Open the aperture wide for the opposite effect: the shutter speed will need to be faster to achieve the same correct exposure.

The size of the aperture opening is often expressed as the f/stop, which is a ratio of the focal length (distance from lens to focus) to the aperture area. The larger the f-stop, the smaller the aperture.

In addition to affecting exposure, the lens aperture controls how much of the foreground and background will be in focus. This is also known as 'depth of field.' A smaller aperture (such as f/22) will result in more of the foreground and background being in focus, also known as having greater depth, or depth of field. Conversely, a larger aperture (such as f/8) will result in less of the foreground and background being in focus, resulting in less depth of field.

A young bull Roosevelt elk, Ecola State Park (Here, a small lens aperture narrowed the depth of field, throwing a greater portion of foreground and background out of focus, making the subject stand out nicely.)

50 Hikes in Oregon

The shutter speed, on the other hand, controls how motion will be interpreted in the image. The shutter speed is measured in fractions of a second. A fast shutter speed will freeze motion with little or no blur on the subject. A slow shutter speed will blur a quickly moving subject. For example, if you are photographing a waterfall and would like to see the individual drops, use a fast shutter speed, perhaps 1/500th of a second, if there is enough light to allow this. If you would like to blur the motion of the water, use a slower shutter speed, perhaps in the 1-second range (keep in mind that slower speeds require the use of a tripod to avoid introducing a blur to the image from an unsteadily held camera).

Both the shutter speed and the aperture are measured in stops. A one-stop change is equal to either doubling or halving the amount of light that reaches the film or chip. For example, a 1/60-second shutter speed is half the speed of 1/125 second and twice the speed of 1/30 second. Each is a one-stop change. In the case of the aperture setting (f/stop), the numbers are a little more awkward to work with, however, the concept is the same. A standard 1-stop aperture series is f/2.8, f/4, f/5.6, f/8, f/11, f/16, and f/22. An aperture setting (f-stop) of f/4 allows half as much light into the camera as f/5.6 does, and twice that of f/2.8. This leads to a useful photographic rule known as reciprocity. An image taken at a shutter speed of 1/60 and f/8 will have the same exposure as one taken at 1/30 and f/5.6, and the same as one taken at 1/125 and f/11. Uses of this rule include adjusting the aperture to shoot moving subjects, such as wildlife, at a higher shutter speed, or increasing the shutter speed to shoot a static subject, such as a landscape, at a lower f-stop to increase the depth of field.

While this may seem like a lot of information to process before you press the shutter, keep in mind that most of today's cameras are capable of doing the calculations for you. Virtually all moderately priced cameras have built-in exposure meters and an array of functions that range from fully automatic to fully manual. Two very useful modes common on most cameras are the aperture priority and shutter priority. Aperture priority mode allows you to set the aperture, and the camera sets the shutter speed. Shutter priority allows you to set the shutter speed, and the camera sets the aperture. These functions can be useful tools when you are trying to determine the optimum depth of field or shutter speed for a particular scene.

One important thing to keep in mind when attempting to determine the correct exposure is that all light meters, and thus the automatic functions of your camera, are preprogrammed to produce the correct exposure of a middle tone (or midtone). Photographers typically refer to middle gray, halfway between black and white, as the middle tone. However, a middle tone does not have to be gray. Some granite rocks, a clear blue sky, lightly faded blue jeans, or the back of your hand can be considered fairly close to a midtone. In many, if not the majority, of situations, your subject or scene will average out to be close to a middle tone. Since your camera's automatic functions are based on the input from the light meter, it should produce a good exposure.

However, when your subject is predominantly dark or light, such as the black obsidian flows in Newberry National Monument or the bright, white snows on Mount Hood, the automatic function of your camera will render the subject as gray. This is because the camera's light meter attempts to average the overall scene as a midtone. In these circumstances, it is best to override the camera's exposure and set the exposure yourself. For example, the snow on Mount Hood may require you to increase the exposure 1½ to 2 stops. If the camera returned an exposure of 1/250 at f/16, decreasing the shutter speed to 1/60 at f/16 or increasing aperture to f/8 at 1/250 would be increasing the exposure 2 stops. The opposite is true for dark subjects, which may require you to decrease the exposure. A general rule of thumb is to add light to light subjects and dark to dark subjects.

Light

While we may be able to adjust the exposure to accommodate some lighting conditions, there is no substitute for photographing in the good light provided by Mother Nature. It is best to avoid shooting in the harsh, high-contrast, mid-day sunlight. This bright light has the effect of washing out colors, and the high contrast hides the details in the shade. The best light occurs in the early morning hours near sunrise and the late afternoon hours near sunset. These times offer a softer and more diffused light, which provides better color saturation and much less contrast and allows details to emerge from the shadows. This is particularly important when photographing in the desert and among the rock formations of eastern Oregon.

In the tall forests of the Coast Range and Cascades, or within the deep canyons and gorges throughout the state, it is often too dark to shoot at sunrise or sunset. In these instances, it may be necessary to wait for the sun to rise higher in the sky. However, this also increases the chances of bright spots of sun appearing on the subject. When this occurs, try to compose the image so these bright or "hot" spots are not included in the image. An overcast sky is often the best time to photograph in these areas. However, be careful not to include the sky as it will look dull and distract from the overall image.

It also important to keep an eye on the environmental conditions of the area you are photographing. For example, due to forest fires and the burning of grass-seed fields, smoke often fills the air of the Cascades and mid-Willamette Valley during the summer and fall. While this may make for some colorful sunsets, it can be a hindrance when attempting to photograph a wide-angle landscape or when using a telephoto lens.

Composition

Once you have determined the best lighting conditions and proper exposure, take your time and compose your photograph carefully. Check the horizon to make sure it is level and that the background is free of any unwanted items that will distract from the main subject. If your camera is equipped with a zoom lens, use it; zoom in and out several times to ensure you have the composition you want and that you are not including any unwanted elements. Try to get as close to the subject as possible and fill the frame. You can do this by either physically moving closer to the subject or by using a zoom lens. This has the effect of simplifying the image and focuses the attention on the subject of the photo. Also keep in mind that most 35mm cameras and digital SLRs do not have 100 percent coverage through the viewfinders. After you have your composition set, zoom in a few more millimeters to avoid including the power line or handrail you carefully positioned just out of the frame.

Film and memory

If you are using film, choose a slower speed film with an ISO rating of 100 or 200. These films typically provide you with greater color saturation and less grain, which is important if you wish to enlarge your image later. This same principle also applies to digital cameras. Choose a setting equivalent to an ISO rating of 100 to 200 and shoot at the highest resolution possible. This may require carrying an extra memory card or two; however, the results are well worth the investment.

Tools

There are a few accessories you may also wish to carry. The first is a tripod. There are many small, lightweight models on the market that can be easily carried or will fit into a daypack. A tripod is essential when photographing in dim light such as that commonly encountered in the heavily forested areas of the Coast Range and Cascades. A general rule of thumb is to always use a tripod when shooting with shutter speeds below 1/60 second and when the shutter speeds are less then the inverse of the focal length you are using. An example would be if you are using a 200mm lens, use a tripod if your shutter speed is less than 1/200 second.

A circular polarizing lens is also an extremely useful item to have in the camera bag. Most of us are familiar with the bluing effects a polarizing lens has on the sky and the removing of reflections from water. However, foliage also reflects light and using a polarizer will remove the reflection and increase the color saturation.

A second filter to consider carrying is a light-yellow 81A or 81B warming filter. These filters (the 81B is slightly darker than the 81A) help remove the bluish tint often seen when photographing in the shade.

GEARING UP FOR THE TRAIL

Depending on the season and/or region of the state you plan to hike, your needs will vary greatly. There are, however, several items that are necessities regardless where you go. These include:

- a sturdy, comfortable pair of shoes (preferably hiking boots) and a dry pair of socks.
- a good, strong water bottle
- extra food such as energy bars or trail mix
- sunscreen
- a knife
- a small hiking first aid kit
- a reliable map and compass

If you intend to hike in the higher elevations remember that the weather can change rapidly, and with snow being possible in any season you may want to consider the following:

- waterproof matches and fire starter
- a flashlight
- an extra shirt and/or rain jacket

When trekking in Oregon's desert regions, be sure to triple the amount of water you usually carry due to the extreme temperature variations. You should also carry an extra long-sleeve shirt, not only to protect you from the sun but also to provide extra warmth if your hike takes you into the evening.

Before leaving on any hike, it is important to let someone know where you intend to go and when you intend to return.

PRECAUTIONS

Potable Water

Many of the trails pass by pristine streams and lakes, and while they may appear pure, every stream is a potential source of the microorganism *Giardia lambli*. The giardia organism is readily spread to surface water through the feces of animals and infected humans. Giardia causes severe diarrhea and dehydration. Water can be made safe by either boiling it for at least 5 minutes or by passing it through a filter with a mesh with openings no wider than 2 microns.

Weather

The greatest hazard to hikers is the weather. Before setting out on any trip, check the weather forecast for the area. Weather can change quickly in the mountain regions of the state. When hiking in the mountains always carry extra food and clothing. Hikers should also not underestimate the effects of the heat. Dehydration can set in rapidly when hiking in the desert regions. When hiking in extreme heat, always carry sunscreen and, as a general rule of thumb, triple the amount of water you would normally carry.

Bears/Mountain Lions

Many of the trails described in this book bring the reader into wilderness areas populated by mountain lion and black bear. While the probability of having an encounter with a mountain lion is extremely rare, it does occur from time to time. In the unlikely event that you do have an encounter, the current wisdom is to act as aggressively as possible in order to scare it off. Remain standing and do not attempt to run. Running may trigger the bear's predatory instinct.

The best way to avoid an encounter with a black bear is to store food securely. In the absence of a bear-proof container, hang your food from a tree. The food should be at least 10 feet above the ground and 6 feet away from the tree. In the rare event that you have an encounter with a black bear, you should remain still and avoid eye contact. If the bear should attack, do not fight back and curl into a ball using your hands to protect the back of your neck. As with a mountain lion, do not run since running may trigger the cat's predatory instinct.

Poison Oak

Poison oak *(Rhus diversiloba)* can be found throughout Oregon and the western United States, where its range extends from Washington south to Baja, California, and east to Arizona. Its habitat includes shady to open woodlands, thickets, and along streambeds. As a crawling shrub, it can cover a very broad area and reach a height of 6 feet; as a climbing vine, it can reach high into the trees. It can be identified by its reddish green, oval-shaped, and almost oily-looking leaves. Poison oak secretes an oily sap that may cause a painful and itchy rash; to individuals who are more sensitive to the sap, the rash may produce blisters and a severe burning sensation. If you suspect you have come in contact with poison oak, even with just your clothing, do not touch the affected area as the oil may be spread to other areas. Remove the affected clothing and place it in a plastic bag or wrap it in a towel to keep it away from other items. Thoroughly wash the area affected with a strong soap in cool water. If the irritation continues for an extended period of time or symptoms become more severe, consult a physician.

A PRECIOUS LEGACY

One of Oregon's most valuable natural resources is its wilderness, which provides, among many things, great scenic beauty. It is the responsibility of all individuals who venture into these areas to maintain and protect these natural assets. By following a few basic principles, we can all help ensure that this precious legacy will be protected for the enjoyment of future generations:

- Whenever possible, walk on preexisting trails and roads and do not cut across switchbacks.
- Camp in preexisting campsites and at least 100 yards away from lakes.
- Bring an extra plastic bag so you can pack out all garbage, even refuse left behind by previous hikers or campers.
- Don't pick flowers or cut down trees, even dead ones, for use as firewood or for any purpose whatsoever.

HOW TO USE THIS BOOK

50 Hikes in Oregon is organized so it's easy to get all the information you need to take off on the trip of your choice. For each hike there is a listing of basic facts, followed by directions to the trailhead and a detailed description of the hike itself.

Trail distances are given in round-trip miles. The estimated hiking times are based upon my actual time hiking the trails while photographing. This often required my carrying a tripod and 30 pounds of camera equipment, so your times may vary. The hike times also incorporate the terrain to be traveled; high-elevation hikes will take longer than those along the coastline. The elevation gain from the trailhead to the highest or lowest point is also provided. While this statistic is a good, rough estimate on the difficulty of the hike, the figure can be deceptive. A trail that contains a lot of small hills may average out to have a greater total elevation gain than a trail that is mostly flat with one, high-elevation climb. The topographical maps included for each hike are particularly helpful when planning the hike.

Each hike also includes a basic rating: easy, moderate, or difficult. These ratings are based on three factors: the length of the trail, the terrain covered, and the elevation. The basic information also includes a recommendation for best seasons to hike the trail. It is based on such variables as trail access, wildflower blooms, wildlife migration, or typical weather conditions.

All the hikes described in the book are on public land or on land owned by organizations that grant public access to the trails, such as The Nature Conservancy. All the trails included in the book are primarily for hiking. None of the hikes permit motorized vehicles. A few of the trails permit mountain bikes, and in the case of hikes in the Eagle Cap Wilderness Area, you may be required to share the trail with horses. While many of the trails allow pets, it is advisable to check with the local authorities regarding specific rules and regulations. When hiking with pets on any of the trails described in this book, remember that leashes are required.

Varying rules and regulations apply in the different land management districts and organizations, so it is always a good idea to check their rules and regulations before hiking the area. This is particularly important when you intend to camp.

ADDRESSES

Deschutes National Forest
1645 US 20 East
Bend, OR 97701
541-383-5300
www.fs.fed.us/r6/centraloregon

Mount Hood National Forest
16400 Champion Way
Sandy, OR 97055
503-668-1700
www.fs.fed.us/r6/mthood

'Ochoco National Forest
3160 N.E. 3rd Street
Prineville, OR 97754
541-416-6500
www.fs.fed.us/r6/centraloregon

Siuslaw National Forest
4077 SW Research Way
Corvallis, OR 97333
541-750-7000
www.fs.fed.us/r6/siuslaw

Umpqua National Forest
2900 NW Stewart Parkway
P.O. Box 1008
Roseburg, OR 97440
541-672-6601
www.fs.fed.us/r6/umpqua

Wallowa-Whitman National Forest
1550 Dewey Avenue
P.O. Box 907
Baker City, OR 97814
541-523-6391
www.fs.fed.us/r6/w-w

Willamette National Forest
P.O. Box 10607
Eugene, OR 97440
541-225-6300
www.fs.fed.us/r6/williamette

Crater Lake National Park
P.O. Box 7
Crater Lake, OR 97604
541-594-3100
www.nps.gov/crla

Oregon Parks and Recreation Department
725 Summer Street NE, Suite C
Salem, OR 97301
800-551-6949
www.prd.state.or.us

Bureau of Land Management (BLM)
Oregon State Office
333 SW 1st Avenue
P.O. Box 2965
Portland, OR 97204
503-808-6002
www.or.blm.gov

Columbia River Gorge National Scenic Area
902 Wasco Avenue, Suite 200
Hood River, OR 97031
541-386-2333
www.fs.fed.us/r6/columbia

Hells Canyon National Recreation Area
88401 OR 82
Enterprise, OR 97828
541-426-4978
www.fs.fed.us/hellscanyon

National Historic Oregon Trail
Interpretive Center
22267 OR 86
P.O. Box 987
Baker City, OR 97814-0987
541-523-1843
www.or.blm.gov/nhotic

John Day Fossil Beds National Monument
32651 OR 19
Kimberly, OR 97848-9701
541-987-2333
www.nps.gov.joda

The Nature Conservancy—Oregon Field Office
821 SE 14th Avenue
Portland, OR 97214
503-230-1221
E-mail: oregon@tnc.org

I

Coast and Coast Range

Wild Oregon iris

More than any other natural feature in the state, it is the coastline that is most associated with Oregon. Unparalleled in its natural beauty, the Oregon coastline stretches for more than 300 miles from the California border near Brookings to the mouth of the Columbia River near Astoria. Massive sand dunes, secluded beaches, picturesque lighthouses, and rugged rock headlands create a scenic paradise for hikers of all ages and abilities.

The coast draws millions of visitors each year; however, most visitors only get out of their cars at the designated scenic pullouts and waysides. Even during the peak tourist months of June, July, and August, many of the longer trails, or those in the Coast Range, remain relatively unpopulated.

One of the most unique features of the Oregon coast has nothing to do with its scenic beauty, but rather its progressive beach-access laws. In 1911 Oregon governor Oswald West designated the state's coastline a public highway, thus preserving access to all of the 262 miles of beaches and 64 miles of headlands.

In 1966 Governor Tom McCall further strengthened the right to public access by passing Oregon's "Beach Bill," which guarantees the public the right to use the dry sand beach along the entire coast. A state easement exists up to the line of vegetation. Only one other state, Hawaii, guarantees public access from the surf line to the vegetation line.

Climate

The Coast Range is by far the region that receives the most precipitation in the state, with areas at the higher elevations and coastal headlands receiving an annual precipitation approaching 100 inches. That being said, the majority of this precipitation occurs during the winter months, leaving the summer months relatively dry. Temperatures are moderate throughout the year with winter temperatures in the 50s or 60s and summer temperatures in the 60s or 70s. Morning fog is a frequent visitor along the coastline during the summer months, but usually burns off by the late morning or afternoon.

Precautions

Before you venture out onto the beach or tide pools, it is advisable to check the local tide tables. Incoming tides can rapidly isolate rocks from headlands and the shore, stranding unsuspecting hikers. Avoid the temptation of strolling out to an interesting rock without knowing when the tide will roll back in. Free tide tables are available at state park offices, information centers, and many shops and motels.

Always keep an eye on the ocean. "Sneaker" waves, unusually large and powerful waves, can appear without warning, even on calm days, and are impossible to predict.

Take care when wading along the beach, as strong currents and undertows are common and quickly sweep unwary beachcombers and waders off their feet and out to sea.

Driftwood is common along the shoreline, much of which is waterlogged timber often weighing several tons, which could easily crush an individual. Each year a number of people are injured in such accidents. Do not attempt to climb on driftwood stacks or even individual logs.

Attractions

In 1970, in order to protect colonies of nesting seabirds and mammals, the U.S. Congress designated all of Oregon's coastal islands and sea stacks off limits to public access, thus creating the Oregon

Islands Wilderness Area. While direct access is prohibited, there are many places along the coast to observe nesting activity without disturbing the wildlife. These include Boardman State Park, Cape Sebastian, Cape Blanco, Coquille Point, Heceta Head, Cape Perpetua, Seal Rock, Yaquina Head, Cascade Head, Cape Meares, and Ecola State Park.

Located just 4 miles west of Astoria is the Fort Clatsop National Memorial. In the winter of 1805 to 1806 this was the winter home of Lewis and Clark and the Corps of Discovery. Interactive exhibits and demonstrations tell the story of daily life at the fort, as well as of the overall expedition. In preparation for the expedition's bicentennial, several new trails have also been constructed.

In 1966, local volunteers purchased 270 acres of land on Cascade Head and donated it to The Nature Conservancy to protect its sensitive plants and wildlife. The preserve is home to native prairie grasses and rare wildflowers. It is also one of only five locations in the world that are home to the threatened Oregon silverspot butterfly. The preserve is located just 1 mile north of Lincoln City and offers several hiking options.

The Yaquina Head Outstanding Natural Area is located 3 miles north of Newport and is home to the Yaquina Head Lighthouse. Built in 1872 and standing 93 feet, it is Oregon's tallest lighthouse and is open to the public for tours from 9 AM to 4 PM daily during the summer and 12 PM to 4 PM during the winter. Yaquina Head also offers an interpretive center that delves into the geology, cultural, human, and natural history of the area.

Two tide pool areas, Cobble Beach and the all-accessible Quarry Cove tide pool, offer the opportunity to observe the local intratidal sea life. A viewpoint next to the lighthouse also provides an eye-level view of nesting seabirds on the rocks (Oregon Islands Wilderness Area) just offshore.

Located near the south end of Newport's historic Yaquina Bay Bridge is the Oregon Coast Aquarium. Once home to Keiko, the killer whale movie star; the tank in which he was once housed has been converted into a dramatic exhibit where visitors pass through a submerged 200-foot acrylic tunnel while large sharks and rays pass both above and below. Other exhibits include a large seabird aviary, sea otters, seals and sea lions, and jellyfish, exploring the various aspects of Oregon's coastal ecosystem.

Five miles north of Florence is the Darlingtonia Wayside, an 18-acre Oregon state park dedicated to the protection of a single plant species, the California pitcher plant, or cobra lily (Darlingtonia californica). Following the trail through a small cedar grove and picnic area, you soon come to a boardwalk that crosses a bog filled with the carnivorous plant. Resembling a bright green cobra about to strike, these unique plants attract insects into their "throat" with a sweet-smelling nectar. The insects are then trapped by downward facing hairs and digested by the plant.

The Oregon Dunes Overlook is located 10 miles north of Reedsport and offers the opportunity to glimpse a portion of the largest expanse of coastal sand dunes in North America. The Oregon Dunes National Recreation Area extends 40 miles along the coastline from the town of Florence to Coos Bay.

Formed by wind and water, some of the largest dunes can reach a height of 500 feet and extend for well over a mile in length. Several hiking options exist within the Recreation Area, for more information stop by the Oregon Dunes Visitor Center, located in Reedsport, which also includes natural and cultural history exhibits.

Located 4 miles north of Brookings and extending for 12 miles along the southern coastline is Boardman State Park. The park encompasses 300-year-old Sitka spruce trees and a maze of sea stacks and natural arches. Several short trails explore the park, with many offering views of the rocky islands just offshore and nesting colonies of seabirds.

1

Saddle Mountain

Location: Saddle Mountain State Natural Area

Distance (round-trip): 5½ miles

Time (one-way): 5 hours

Vertical rise: 1,620 feet

Difficulty: difficult

Map: USGS 7½' Saddle Mountain

Best season: spring, summer, fall

At 3,283 feet, Saddle Mountain would not seem to be much of a mountain. Halfway up the steep, switchbacking 2¾-mile trail you may begin to change your mind. However, the visual rewards at the summit make the effort worth it. On a clear spring day the endless blue sky and panoramic views of the distant Cascades and Pacific Ocean contrasts with the many wildflowers along the trail.

Getting There

From Portland travel east on US 26 for 65 miles and turn right at the SADDLE MOUNTAIN STATE PARK sign onto Saddle Mountain Road. Follow Saddle Mountain Road 7 miles to its end at the walk-in campground parking area where a sign marks the trailhead.

Special Notes

Do not attempt the summit in snow or icy conditions. The many steep drop-offs and cliffs make this trail unsuitable for small children or pets. Wildflower picking is strictly prohibited. No permits or access fees are required.

The Trail

Saddle Mountain has its origins 250 miles to the east and 15 million years in the past. Near the Idaho border large fissures in the earth's crust began a series of eruptions creating what is now known as the Columbia River Basalt Flows. Saddle Mountain is a remnant of some of the last of these flows as it met the Pacific Ocean.

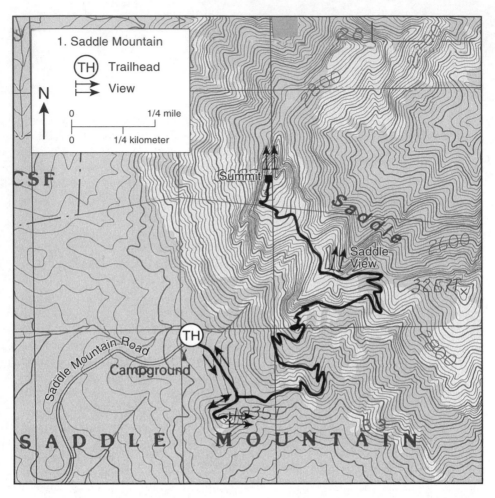

When the lava encountered the cold water, it cooled quite rapidly and, in some instances, explosively, creating cracks and fractures. The still-fluid lava following was then forced into and through the cracks, forming the patterns seen now in the rock along the trail. As the land rose and the ocean receded, the elements eroded the surrounding softer sedimentary rock exposing these features of the mountain.

The trail begins at the small 10-site primitive walk-in campground. Reservations are not accepted and sites are allocated on a first-come, first-served basis, so if you wish to camp during the summer months it is a good idea to arrive early on a Friday or plan a midweek trip. The trail continues through second-growth fir and alder, passing stumps from logging activities of the 1920s. After ¼ mile you encounter an unmarked junction. For the best overall view of the mountain, follow the right fork. The trail leads ¼ mile through moss-covered Douglas fir and around a small rock outcropping. The last few feet of this trail leads up a steep trail carved into the rock. The footing is a bit tricky, so use the cable handrail. As you reach the broad flat top,

Saddle Mountain from the viewpoint

you will be treated with a great view of both the east and west peaks of Saddle Mountain. Return as you came to continue to the summit of Saddle Mountain.

As you continue along, the main trail becomes steeper and you begin to switchback up 1 mile to a basalt dike on the south peak. The dike was created when the still fluid portions of the lava forced its way down through the cracks and fissures of the already solidified basalt. After another ½ mile you come to the wildflower meadows on the upper slopes of the lower south peak. Use the wooden walkways when passing through this area to avoid damaging the fragile meadows.

During the spring and early summer months, Saddle Mountain is home to a variety of rare wildflower species, including the white-flowered and low-growing Saddle Mountain alpine bittercress and the chocolate lily with its mottled dark purple flowers.

The mountain offers the only alpine habitat in the northwest portion of the state and is the basis of the Saddle Mountain State Natural Area. The habitat acts is a refuge to the wildflowers of the last Ice Age that have long since disappeared from northwestern Oregon. Other species you are likely to see along the trail include paintbrush, iris, larkspur, trillium, copper bush, monkeyflower, penstemon, catchfly, asters, and phlox. Picking any of the flowers on the mountain is prohibited, so please avoid the temptation and leave them for those who will follow.

Continuing for another ¼ mile brings you to the mountain's saddle. A cable handrail offers some reassurance as you cross this narrow section, which offers a vertiginous view of the park, 1,500 feet below.

From the saddle it's a little less than ½ mile to the summit. Another cable handrail anchored into the rock offers some assistance to the summit. On a clear day the railed viewpoint provides panoramic views of the Pacific Ocean, the mouth of the Columbia River, and the Astoria Bridge to the west. The distant Olympic Range is visible to the north and to the east lies the snow-covered peaks of Mount Rainier, Mount St. Helens, Mount Adams, and Mount Hood.

2

Ecola State Park

Location: 2 miles north of Cannon Beach

Distance (round-trip): 6½ miles

Time (round-trip): 5 hours

Vertical rise: 800 feet

Difficulty: moderate

Maps: USGS 7½' Tillamook Head; Ecola State Park brochure

Best season: spring, summer, fall

Between two of Oregon's more popular coastal communities—Seaside to the north and Cannon Beach to the south—lies an oasis containing some of the most beautiful scenery along the Oregon coastline.

Getting There
From Cannon Beach follow the ECOLA STATE PARK signs 2 miles to the park entrance. Turn left just past the entrance booth and follow the road to the picnic area parking lot.

Special Notes
An Oregon State Park day-use fee is required to park at the trailhead and is available at the parking lot ($3 daily).

The Trail
Before beginning the hike, take some time to walk the ¼-mile path to the Ecola Point viewing platform. From here you can look south to the city of Cannon Beach and at Haystack Rock. The view north includes Tillamook Head Lighthouse and allows you to survey the trail's terrain down to Indian Beach and back up to your destination at Tillamook Head. As with most of the northern headlands, Tillamook Head and the surrounding sea stacks are composed of 15-million-year-old Columbia River Basalt.

The Tillamook Rock lighthouse, or "Terrible Tilly," as she was known to those who served on her, was completed in 1881, just three weeks too late to save the British ship *Lupatia* when it ran aground on Tillamook Head. Built at a cost of $125,000 the 62-foot-high tower housed a first-order

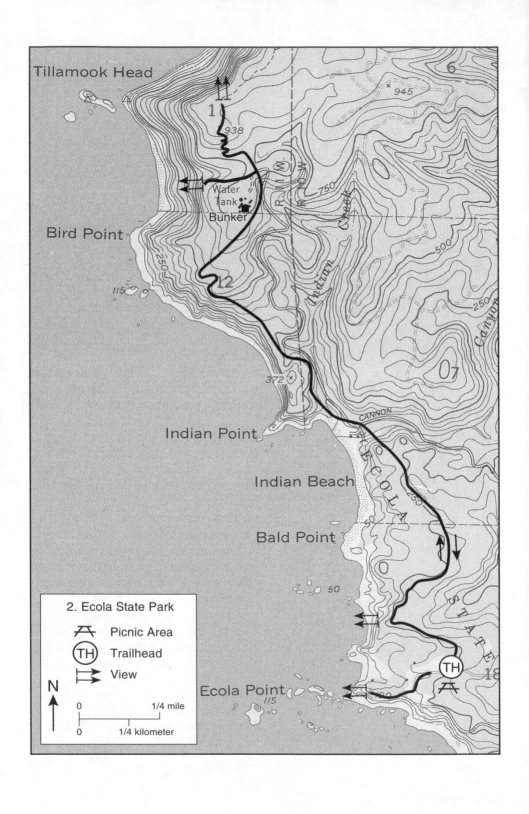

Tillamook Head

*945

938

Bird Point

Water
Tank
Bunker

750

Indian Creek

500

115

250

12

250

Canyon

372 ×

07

CANNON

Indian Point

ECOLA

Indian Beach

250

Bald Point

50

STATE

50

50

2. Ecola State Park

Picnic Area

TH   Trailhead

View

N

Ecola Point

115

TH

18

0   1/4 mile
0   1/4 kilometer

Indian Beach, Ecola State Park

Fresnel lens displayed 130 feet above sea level. Over the years many modifications have been made to the structure to protect it from the violent storms that frequent the area. On several stormy occasions, rocks weighing in excess of 100 pounds have been literally hurled into the lighthouse tower. The lighthouse was decommissioned in 1957. It was purchased in 1980 by a private organization (in cooperation with the state) and converted into Eternity at Sea Columbarium. In 1994, the U.S. Congress designated Tillamook Rock a Federal Wildlife Refuge, home to nesting common murres, cormorants, and other species.

The trailhead to Tillamook Head is located at the northeast end of the Ecola Point parking area. From here the trailheads north and climbs up and along the fir- and spruce-covered bluffs. Although Ecola State Park is relatively small and located between two of the coast's busiest towns, both black bear and elk are frequent visitors to the park. On the route down to Indian Beach, you will encounter several viewpoints along the cliff overlooking Sealion Rock and the Tillamook Lighthouse. After about 1 mile the trail begins to descend toward Indian Beach, the site of an old Native American village, where it crosses Canyon Creek as you enter the Indian Beach Picnic Area.

Take a sunset stroll along Indian Beach and you will soon understand why this is one of the most photographed locations along the Oregon coastline. The rocky cliffs of the headlands, sandy beach, and many sea stacks just offshore provide an abundance of photographic subjects. In 1806, Captain William Clark and 12 members of the Corps of Discovery used this same trail to cross the headland on their way to Cannon Beach to trade with the local natives for the blubber of a beached whale.

Picking up the trail on the north side of the picnic area, stay to the left and ignore tho old service road on the right. The trail immediately crosses Indian Creek and begins a fairly steep climb toward the headland. After 1½ miles you reach a small backpacking camping area and a trail junction.

Turn left and follow the trail for ¼ mile until you come to an old, moss-covered concrete bunker constructed during World War II as a radar installation. Follow the trail a few more yards to a cliff-side viewpoint perched 750 feet above the rocky shoreline where the view extends beyond the Tillamook Rock lighthouse and far out to sea. During the spring and fall, the distinctive spouts of gray whales can be seen as they pass the Tillamook Head on their 12,000-mile migration to and from the warm-water breeding grounds off Baja and the rich feeding grounds in the Bering and Chuckchi Sea.

From here the trail continues along the cliff's edge for another 4¼ miles to Seaside; however, the viewpoint makes a good place to turn back and complete the moderate 6½-mile hike. If you do plan on making the hike down to Seaside, it is a good idea either to start at Indian Beach or arrange for a shuttle to pick you up in Seaside.

3

Oswald West State Park

Location: 10 miles south of Cannon Beach

Distance (round-trip): 7 miles

Time (round-trip): 4½ hours

Vertical rise: 300 feet

Difficulty: moderate

Maps: USGS 7½' Arch Cape; Oswald West State Park brochure

Best season: spring, summer, fall, winter

Vistas overlooking a rocky coastline and a small sand beach that attract surfers from around the state highlight this moderate hike through old-growth cedar and Sitka spruce.

Getting There

From Cannon Beach drive south 10 miles on US 101 to the Oswald West State Park day-use parking area on the left. The trailhead is located near the restrooms at the east end of the parking area.

Special Notes

No permits or access fees are required. A $14 fee is required for camping.

The Trail

Oswald West State Park encompasses approximately 2,500 acres of mostly undeveloped coastline. Located ¼ mile from the parking area along US 101 is a 36-site walk-in campground beside Necarney Creek. Campsites are allocated on a first-come, first-served basis. During the summer months, the campground fills up very quickly on the weekends so either arrive early or plan a weekday trip. Wheelbarrows are provided to assist in hauling camping gear to the campground.

The park is named after Governor Oswald West (1911–1915), whose leadership halted private development and guaranteed public access to all of Oregon's beaches and headlands by declaring them public highways.

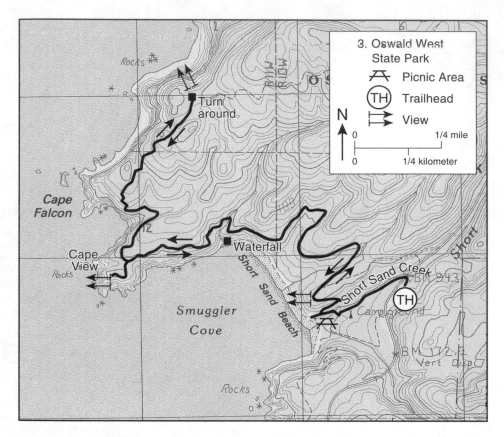

3. Oswald West
State Park
⊼   Picnic Area
(TH) Trailhead
⊢⇒ View
N
0   1/4 mile
0   1/4 kilometer

The trailhead is located on the east end of the day-use parking area along Short Sand Creek. The trail passes under US 101 and continues along the creek, through old-growth cedar, hemlock, and spruce that can reach 12 feet in diameter and 200 feet high. Pass by the first trail on your left, which leads to the walk-in campground, and continue along the creek to the picnic area and the intersection of the Oregon Coast Trail ½ mile from the parking area.

From the picnic area, turn right and follow the Oregon Coast Trail as it winds through a dense growth of salal and spruce toward Cape Falcon. After ½ mile a short trail leads to a bench where you can rest and peer through the trees down upon Short Sand Beach and the surfers in Smugglers Cove.

From the viewpoint the trail retreats back into the forest, passing several boggy areas lined with skunk cabbage. Spring also brings trillium and wild iris. After approximately ¾ mile, the trail emerges onto the rocky cliffs overlooking Smugglers Cove. Below, the incoming surf crashing against the rocks often sends spray 50 feet high or more into the air. The trail soon forks, with the left fork leading a few hundred yards to the salal-covered headlands of Cape Falcon. To the south lie the rocky headlands below the pointed dome of 1,600-foot-high Neahkahnie Mountain.

Clatsop Indian legends tell of a "winged canoe" that anchored off the coast and dispatched a team of men who buried a chest on Neahkahnie Mountain and marked the

Sunset over Short Sand Creek, Oswald State Park

spot with an inscribed rock. The legends remained just that until 1890 when treasure hunter Pat Smith discovered a 200-pound rock not far from Nehalem Beach. The surface of the stone was chiseled with the letter W with a cross on each side, and the letters DE along with eight dots and an arrow pointing up the mountainside. A short distance away, a smaller rock was found with two dots and an arrow pointing back toward the larger stone. The legend was fueled even more when, in the early 1900s, workmen discovered two crude bronze handles that appeared to be handles from a chest; however, no sign of the chest or its contents were ever found. The mystery deepened when, in the 1930s, a local resident found a chunk of beeswax with roman numerals and geometric shapes inscribed on its surface similar to those known to be carried by Spanish galleons.

Although many still roam the mountain and beaches looking for Spanish gold, today it is widely accepted that the beeswax was from a Spanish shipwreck on Nehalem Beach in the early 1700s and the rocks were markers used as part of a survey to stake out a land claim made in the late 1500s. In 1579, Sir Francis Drake claimed all the land above 45 degrees north latitude for England.

As you continue north along the trail through the salal and weathered spruce, you come to several scenic, cliff-edge viewpoints that look west out to sea and north toward Arch Cape and Cannon Beach. After 1 mile you reach the last viewpoint before the trail begins a series of steep switchbacks heading inland. This makes a good point to turn around and head down to the beach where you can take your boots off and cool your feet in the Pacific surf.

To access Short Sand Beach on your return trip, turn right at the picnic area and follow the trail a few hundred feet to the sand stairs. In the spring and winter months, runoff produces a wonderful little waterfall cascading into the surf at the far north end of the beach.

4

Cape Meares State Park

Location: Three Capes Scenic Loop 10 miles west of Tillamook, 26 miles north of Pacific City

Distance (round-trip): 3½ miles combined

Time (round-trip): 3 hours

Vertical gain: 600 feet

Difficulty: moderate

Maps: USGS 7½' Netarts; Oregon State Parks brochure

Best season: spring, summer, fall, winter

Cape Meares is named for the British Sea Captain John Meares who was engaged in the fur trade along the coast of Alaska and British Columbia. In the late 1780s Captain Meares sailed south in search of the Columbia River. He missed sighting the Columbia and turned back north at this point.

Getting There
From Tillamook follow the Three Capes Scenic Route 10 miles west to the Cape Meares State Park entrance on your right. Follow the entrance ½ mile to the parking lot. From Pacific City follow the Three Capes Scenic Route 26 miles north through Oceanside to the Cape Meares State Park entrance on your left.

Special Notes
During the summer season (May through October) the lighthouse and gift shop are open daily 11 AM TO 4 PM. There is no day-use fee.

The Trail
Cape Meares State Park and Cape Meares National Wildlife Refuge offer a nice ½-mile stroll along the cliffs of the cape and lighthouse, as well as a moderate 3-mile hike through the refuge and down to the shore.

An observation platform next to the parking lot offers views south along the coast to Cape Lookout and the National Wildlife Refuge of Three Arch Rocks. Three Arch Rocks was designated a wildlife refuge by Congress in 1970 and was the first wildlife

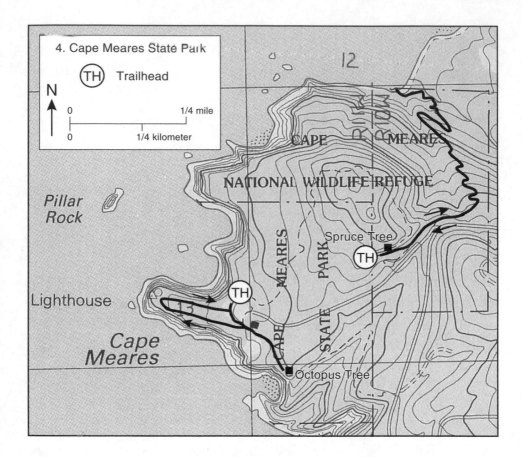

4. Cape Meares State Park

(TH) Trailhead

N

0   1/4 mile

0   1/4 kilometer

12

CAPE   MEARES

NATIONAL WILDLIFE REFUGE

Pillar Rock

Spruce Tree

(TH)

Lighthouse

(TH)

Cape Meares

CAPE MEARES STATE PARK

Octopus Tree

refuge west of the Mississippi River. During the breeding season this tiny refuge is home to more than 200,000 common murres, 2,000 tufted puffins, as well as, hundreds of petrels and cormorants.

From the parking lot, a short trail of a few hundred feet leads past the restroom and to the "Octopus Tree." This old 10-foot-thick Sitka spruce has been contorted by the wind and has six large irregular arms growing from its base. After visiting the tree, turn around and head back to the parking area. The trail continues past the tree, meandering along for another uneventful ½ mile to a turnout along the Three Capes Scenic Route.

The trail to the lighthouse begins at the southwest end of the parking lot. The wide paved trail continues down the cape, through salal and rhododendrons, for ¼ mile where it forks. Bring your binoculars and take your time at the observation points to watch the incoming ocean swells, the sea lions relaxing on the rocks below, or perhaps even a migrating gray whale. The left fork continues to the lighthouse 100 feet away while the right fork loops back to the parking lot.

Built in 1890, this quaint little lighthouse stands only 35 feet tall, however, its position on the cape elevates it to 220 feet above the Pacific. The Cape Mears Lighthouse was originally scheduled to be built on Cape Lookout 15 miles south. However, due to a map error, construction began at Cape

The cliffs at Cape Meares State Park

Meares. By the time the mistake was discovered, construction at the Cape Meares site was too far along, and it was declared the official site.

Following the loop, you cross the cape through a dense growth of spruce and salal to the north side. From here the parking lot is only ¼ mile away. Several points along the way offer views of the cliffs to the north and Cape Meares National Wildlife Area.

For a longer hike, drive back to the intersection of the Three Capes Scenic Route and the park, where a small parking area identifies the trailhead to the beach and a giant spruce. A few feet from the trailhead, the trail forks. The left fork leads ¼ mile to an ancient and immense Sitka spruce, 190 feet tall and nearly 50 feet in circumference. Returning on the same path, follow the right fork as it winds its way through the Cape

Meares National Wildlife Area. The trail offers views of Tillamook Bay, the tiny town of Cape Meares, and Bayocean Spit.

In the early 1900s, Bayocean Spit was a bustling resort billed as the "Playground of the Pacific Northwest," boasting a first-class hotel, a bowling alley, a 1,000-seat theater, and a 50-by-160-foot indoor saltwater swimming pool complete with a wave machine. Unfortunately the completion of the North Tillamook Jetty in 1917 changed the ocean currents, and by 1939 erosion of the spit had completely claimed the resort.

Continuing along for another ¾ mile, the trail again forks. The right fork leads to the town of Cape Meares ¾ mile away. Stay to the left and after a short ¼ mile you reach the ocean. During low tide you can scramble down the bank to a wonderful little gravel beach along the cape.

5

Munson Creek Falls

*Location: Munson Creek State Park,
8 miles south of Tillamook, Tillamook
State Forest*

Distance (round-trip): ¾ mile

Time (round-trip): ½ hour

Vertical rise: 100 feet

Difficulty: easy

Map: USGS 7½' Beaver

Best season: spring, summer, fall, winter

At 266 feet, Munson Creek Falls is the tallest waterfall in the Coast Range and the second highest in the state. The creek on which the falls is located is named after Gorgan Munson, an early settler of the area. In 1998 Paul Allen donated the 61 acres of land surrounding Munson Creek Falls to the state of Oregon.

Getting There

From Tillamook, go 8 miles south on US 101 and turn left onto Munson Creek Road. A small sign along US 101 also points the way. After approximately ½ mile, the road turns to gravel. Follow the park signs another mile to Munson Creek State Park, which will be to your right.

Special Notes

The waterfall is at its highest flow in the spring and winter. Foliage may obscure the view in late spring, summer, and early fall. An Oregon State Park day-use fee is required to park at the trailhead and is available at the parking lot ($3 daily).

The Trail

This enjoyable stroll through old-growth fir, cedar, and Sitka spruce and along Munson Creek is really too short to be called a hike. However, this lightly used trail is more than worth the visit.

The wide and well-maintained trail begins at the top end of the park turnaround. The trail follows the creek through large cedar, alder, and maple covered in moss. After ¼ mile the trail ends at the falls' viewpoint. In

Munson Creek Falls and trail

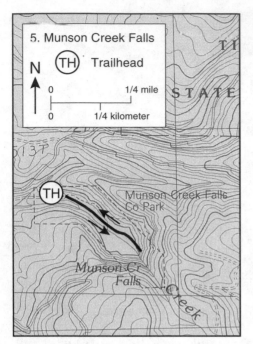

5. Munson Creek Falls

N (TH) Trailhead

0 ——————— 1/4 mile

0 ——————— 1/4 kilometer

Munson Creek Falls Co Park

Munson Cr Falls

Creek

the late spring and early fall, the view of the lower portion of the falls is obscured by the alder, big leaf maple, and vine maple.

A few yards before the end of the trail, an old, unmaintained upper trail forks to the left. This trail is overgrown, and you have to step across a few windfalls but after a few hundred yards the trail ends at a mid-falls viewpoint, which offers a much better view of the falls and canyon below. The original trails were built in the early 1960s as part of a youth conservation program.

On your return trip down the trail, look for wild iris, monkeyflower, salmonberry, and elderberry. The park is also home to the world's second-tallest spruce, which stands 260 feet tall and 8 feet in diameter.

The basalt cliff that creates the falls was originally the sea floor of the Pacific Ocean. It was created by undersea eruptions 15 to 20 million years ago during the Miocene time. Due to the action of the Continental plate passing over the Pacific plate, the ancient sea floor has been exposed.

Keep an eye out for ravens, gulls, and various songbirds that all frequent the area, as do deer and raccoons. The gravel streambed of Munson Creek is also an important spawning ground for salmon.

6

Cape Lookout

Location: Cape Lookout State Park

Distance (round-trip): 4¾ miles

Time (round-trip): 3 hours

Vertical rise: 400 feet

Difficulty: easy

Map: USGS 7½' Sand Lake

Best season: spring, summer, fall, winter

Unlike many of Oregon's prominent coastal points, Cape Lookout juts far out into the Pacific, offering spectacular views to the north and the south.

Getting There
From Tillamook turn west onto third Street (Three Capes Scenic Route) and follow the signs to Cape Lookout State Park. Pass the Cape Lookout campground and, after traveling 15¾ miles from Tillamook, turn right at the trailhead sign into the trail parking area.

Special Notes
With an average annual rainfall of 100 inches, it's wise to bring a rain jacket. Even during the summer months, portions of the trail may be muddy. An Oregon State Park day-use pass is required to park at the trailhead and is available at the parking lot ($3 daily).

The Trail
Like most of the headlands on the north Oregon coast, Cape Lookout is composed of 15-million-year-old Columbia River Basalt originating 300 miles to the east. The unique shape of the cape is a result of the several lava flows filling a small coastal valley, creating a basalt cast. Time, weather, and the relentless Pacific have long ago washed away the surrounding valley walls.

The trail begins at the far west end of the parking area. Follow the left trail where, after a few hundred yards, the south section of the Oregon Coast Trail joins from the left. Stay to the right to continue down the cape.

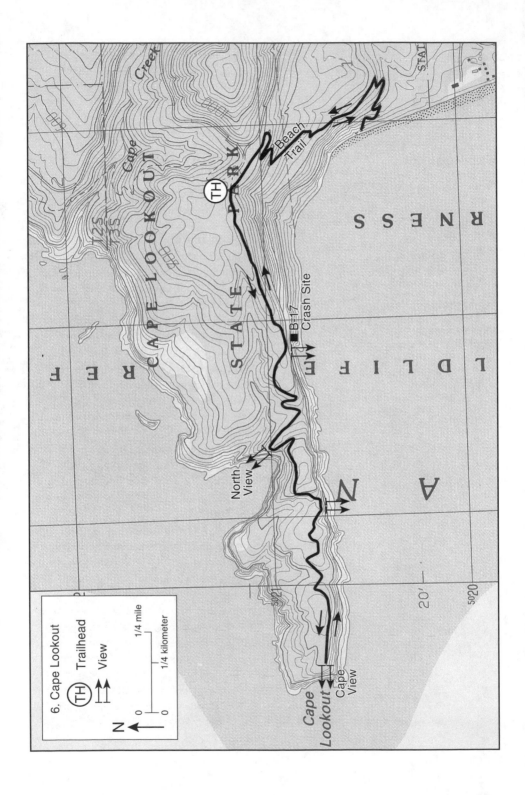

6. Cape Lookout

TH Trailhead

View

N

0   1/4 mile
0   1/4 kilometer

Cape Lookout

Cape View

North View

B-17 Crash Site

Beach Trail

CAPE LOOKOUT STATE PARK

WILDERNESS

REF

Cape Creek

12S
13S

20'

5020

5021

Cape Lookout view, looking north

After a little more than ½ mile you reach a railed viewpoint where a small bronze memorial plaque in the cliff marks the 1943 crash site of a B-17 bomber on patrol over the Pacific Coast. From here the view extends south to Cape Kiwanda, Cascade Head, and Cape Foulweather. Continuing on the trail leads back into the dense spruce and hemlock forest as it crosses over to the northern side of the cape. The undergrowth consists mostly of salal and sword fern. In the spring trillium, candy flower, and rhododendron can also be found along the trail.

You get your first view north at a small, railed viewpoint after approximately 1¼ miles into the hike. Peering through the trees you can see Three Arch Rocks, Cape Mears, and on a clear day, Neahkahanie Mountain.

Continuing on, the trail passes an old slide providing a dizzying view of the sea below. The trail once again crosses over to the south side of the cape and edges along the cliffs. Along this stretch of the trail, you will pass several narrow sections of the trail with dizzying views straight down to the Pacific more than 400 feet below. The trail is often slippery, so use extreme caution when passing by these sections. After another ¾

mile, the trail brings you to the end of the cape where a railed viewpoint and a small meadow lie 400 feet above the sea. This is a great place to have lunch and, during the months of December through June, watch for the spouts of migrating gray whales as they round the cape on their way to or from Alaska.

If you would like to hike down to the beach on your return trip, turn right at the junction with the Oregon Coast Trail. Follow the steep path as it switchbacks down the cliff 1¾ miles to the beach. The first 2 miles of the beach are off-limits to motorized traffic, after which you enter the Sand Lake Recreation Area, a very popular off-road area.

From the parking area, the right-hand trail leads to the campground 2½ miles away. This trail winds its way through the old-growth forest and offers several views of the north side of the cape, Sphinx Island, and associated sea stacks. The campground is located on the sand spit between Netarts Bay and the Pacific Ocean. The park offers several miles of beach to comb and is reputedly a good place to find glass fishing floats. The campground has more than 200 camping sites, 13 yurts, and 3 cabins. Rates range from $12 to $65 per night.

7

Drift Creek Falls

Location: Siuslaw National Forest

Distance (round-trip): 3 miles

Time (round-trip): 2 hours

Vertical rise: 350 feet

Difficulty: easy

Map: USGS 7½' Drift Creek

Best season: spring, summer, fall, winter

The highlight of this trail is the 100-foot-high suspension bridge that crosses the creek just above Drift Creek Falls.

Getting There

From Portland follow US 18 west toward Lincoln City. Five miles before reaching US 101, turn left onto Bear Creek Road (Forest Service Road 17). Continue on Bear Creek Road for 3½ miles where it turns into Forest Service Road 17. Continue straight on Road 17 for another 7 miles to the paved parking area on the right. From Lincoln City, travel east on US 18 for 5 miles until you reach Bear Creek Road on your right.

Special Notes

Even during the summer months portions of the trail may be muddy. A Northwest Forest Pass is required to park at the trailhead and is available from many private vendors ($5 daily, $30 annually).

The Trail

The trailhead is located just to the left of the information board on the south end of the parking area. The trail begins with a gradual descent through a dense forest of Douglas fir and western hemlock on its way down to the creek. Sword fern and bracken fern, along with vine maple and salal, make up the majority of the understory. Early spring also brings blooming trillium and the clover-like oxalis with its tiny white flowers.

Approximately ½ mile down the trail a wooden footbridge crosses a small seasonal creek, which is then followed by a newly constructed, but as yet uncompleted, trail that leads to the right. Stay to the left and after another ½ mile you gradually descend to a beautiful creek winding through alder, vine maple, and a few western red cedar. After following the creek for 100 yards the trail crosses the creek on a wooden footbridge and then skirts a 25-year-old clear-cut before entering an old-growth forest of hemlock, Douglas fir, and cedar. If you are hiking the trail close to sunset you may get a glimpse of a spotted owl. The old-growth forest along Drift Creek is known to have a large population of these controversial little owls.

A little more than ¼ mile from the creek brings you to the edge of the Drift Creek Canyon and the magnificent suspension bridge. The bridge was completed in 1997 and is dedicated to Scott Paul who lost his life on the project. The bridge is 240 feet in length, 30 inches wide, and crosses 100 feet above Drift Creek. While it may look delicate, the bridge is strong enough to support 80 tons!

A small picnic area on the opposite side is a nice place to rest, have lunch, and view the falls. For a better view of the falls, follow the trail past the picnic area for a short ¼ mile down to the creek bank. From here you can view the thin, 75-foot-high ribbon of the falls as it plunges into the pool below the bridge.

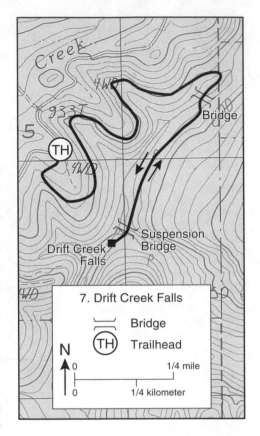

7. Drift Creek Falls

⌣ Bridge

(TH) Trailhead

N

0   1/4 mile

0   1/4 kilometer

Drift Creek Falls and bridge

8

Cape Perpetua

Location: Cape Perpetua Scenic Area

Distance (round-trip): 4¾ miles

Time (one-way): 3 hours

Vertical rise: 400 feet

Difficulty: easy

Map: USGS 7½' Yachats

Best season: spring, summer, fall, winter

Three short hikes explore the 2,700-acre Cape Purpetua Scenic Area's spruce forest, beach, tide pools, and breathtaking views north and south along the coastline.

Getting There

From Yachats travel south 3 miles on US 101 and turn left at the Cape Perpetua Visitor Center.

Special Notes

When exploring the rocks near the chasms, use extreme caution. The areas near the chasms are not recommended for small children.

A day-use fee is required to park at the trailhead and is payable at the parking lot ($3 daily).

The Trail

In 1778, while sailing up the coast, the famed explorer Captain Cook encountered fierce headwinds. For five days his ship was unable to make any headway. On March 11, the day honoring Saint Perpetua, the captain irritably noted that the cape was perpetually in view. Whether out of spite, or in honor, the name stuck.

All three trails begin at the Cape Perpetua Visitor Center. The first trail is a short, 2-mile stroll along Cape Creek to an extremely large and old Sitka spruce. After viewing the exhibits in the center, turn left and follow the trail down to a junction. Stay to the right and follow the Giant Spruce Trail as it joins Cape Creek. The wide gravel trail makes its way through the alder and

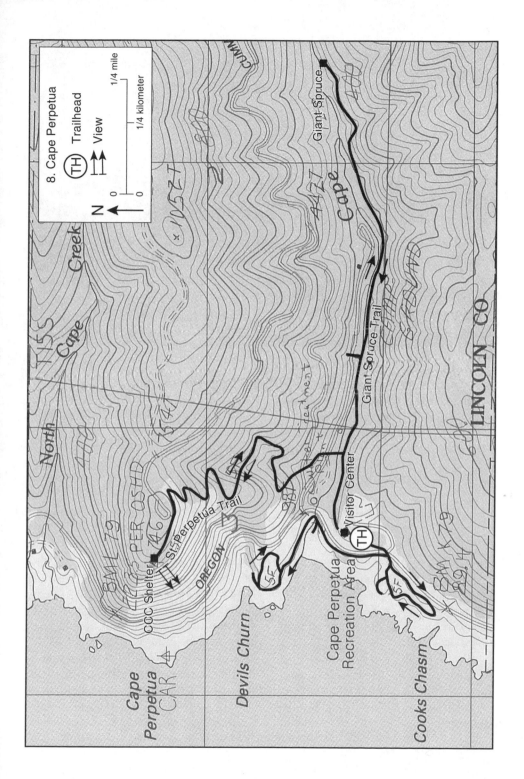

Devils Churn, Cape Perpetua

giant spruce, many of them more than 10 feet in diameter, as it passes just opposite the creek from the campground. Skunk cabbage, foxglove, and wild iris are some of the wildflowers growing along the trail. After a mile you reach the contorted, 500-year-old, 180-foot-tall Sitka spruce.

As you head back down the trail, turn right at the junction just before the visitor center and join the 2½-mile round-trip St. Perpetua Trail. The trail passes over Cape Creek and then crosses the campground road and cape road before beginning a steep climb up to the viewpoint. In addition to the countless number of views, the trail passes through meadows of camas, paintbrush, and foxglove.

After 1¼ miles and numerous switchbacks, you arrive at the stone shelter built in the early 1930s by the Civilian Conservation Corps (CCC). From 750 feet above the Pacific, the views extend north to Cape Foulweather and on a clear day south

to Heceta Head and Cape Blanco, a distant 100 miles away.

The third trail again begins at the visitor center and follows a paved trail through a tunnel underneath US 101. Turn left and follow the trail around the loop to Cooks Chasm and the Spouting Horn. At high tide the waves enter a small underwater cave, which sends the water high into the air.

As you return and rejoin the Restless Waters Trail you will cross a small footbridge. Embedded in the bank along the bridge, you will notice numerous layers of shells. This is the remains of a shell midden, or shell mound, created by the Alsi Native Americans who used the area as a summer camp 500 to 1,500 years ago.

Continuing along you soon come to a short trail spur to the left that roughly parallels Cape Creek down to the sandy beach and tide pools. The sea often piles driftwood at the base of the trail, so use extreme caution when crossing to the beach. The well-developed tide pools are filled with mussels, barnacles, snails, hermit crabs, anemones, urchins, sea stars, and sculpins.

Following the main trail, you soon come to another trail junction as you pass through a small stand of alder. Stay left and follow the trail along the north side of the cape where you enter a small forest of short, twisted Sitka spruce. The trail climbs slightly as it curves around the point to a viewpoint overlooking Devils Churn, a chasm still being created by the relentless erosion of the ocean waves along a fracture in the lava. A short spur to the left leads down to the churn where you can experience the full power of the Pacific up close. Use extreme caution and stay well back from the chasm as the spray from the incoming waves and algae make the ledge slippery.

Back on the main trail, you continue making your way through the spruce to another junction. The right fork leads back to the Restless Waters Trail and the visitor center, while the left fork leads to the Devils Churn parking area with restrooms and a small concession stand.

9

Heceta Head

Location: US 101 12 miles south of Yachats, 15 miles north of Florence

Distance (round-trip): 4½ miles

Time (round-trip): 2½ hours

Vertical gain: 600 feet

Difficulty: moderate

Maps: USGS 7½' Heceta Head; USFS Siuslaw National Forest

Best season: spring, summer, fall, winter

Heceta Head is named for the Spanish explorer Bruno de Heceta, who first sighted the cape in 1775. Built of bricks shipped from San Francisco, the lighthouse first cast its light far out to sea in 1894. Perched above Parrot Rock, named for the now rarely seen puffins and nestled in windswept Sitka spruce, the Heceta Head lighthouse is one of the most photographed lighthouses in the world.

Getting There

From Florence travel north 12 miles on US 101. As you exit the tunnel and cross the bridge, turn left into Devils Elbow State Park. From Yachats, travel south 12 miles on US 101 and turn right into Devils Elbow State Park.

Special Notes

Due to the prominence of the cape, fog is common, and even during the summer months, the trail can be slippery. An Oregon State Park day-use fee is required to park at the trailhead, payable at the parking lot ($3 daily).

The Trail

The parking lot for Devils Elbow State Park is located in the shadows of the 220-foot arch of the Cape Creek Bridge built in 1933. The trail begins at the north end of the parking lot, climbing ¼ mile through salal and spruce to an old service road and the beautiful white, red-roofed assistant lighthouse keeper's residence.

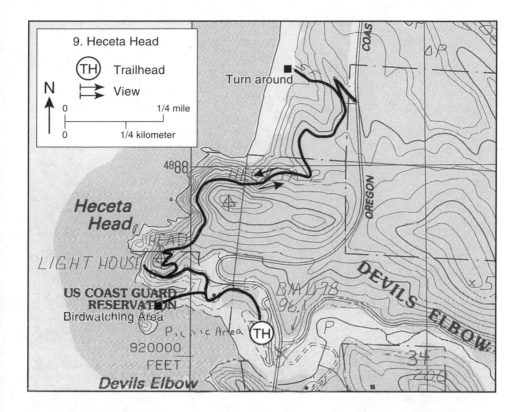

Like many lighthouses, Heceta Head is said to be haunted. The ghost is supposedly a young woman named Rue who some believe is Mrs. Frank DeRay, the wife of an early lighthouse keeper. Mrs. DeRay was a strong-willed and fastidious housekeeper who is said to overlook all repairs and renovations to this day.

From the keeper's house, a short trail of a few hundred yards leads to a small viewing area of Parrot Rock where, in the spring, nesting gulls, common murres (a bird of the order pygopodes, or diving birds, which include loons and puffins), and Brandt's cormorants can be seen in very large numbers. Tufted puffins, now scarce here, were once very common and are the source of Parrot Rock's name.

Following the old service road for another 1/4 mile brings you to the railed grounds of the lighthouse. From the fence line, you can look down onto nesting birds on Parrot Rock. Watch for bald eagles that frequent the area and California pelicans as they round the headland, skimming inches above the incoming ocean swells.

In the summer, tours of the lighthouse are conducted daily by volunteers and are well worth the time, not only for the view of the ocean but for a close-up view of the huge lighthouse lens. The lens is perched upon a 56-foot-high tower and is a first-order Fresnel, composed of 640 hand-ground prisms. Construction began on the lighthouse in 1892 and was completed in 1894. It stands 205 feet above the surf, and its

Hecata Head Lighthouse

light, the brightest on the Oregon coast, is visible for up to 21 miles out to sea.

From the lighthouse, the trail climbs and switchbacks through weathered, wind-swept Sitka spruce and rhododendrons. Spring and summer may also bring wild iris and monkeyflower. As the trail winds its way back toward US 101, stop and enjoy the views north up the coastline to Cape Perpetua.

After 1 1/4 miles, a short spur to the right leads to a small pullout along US 101. Stay to the left and follow Hobbit Trail. As you follow the trail around the switchbacks and through the dense Sitka spruce tunnels, you will understand how the trail obtained its J.R.R. Tolkien–derived name. After 1/2 mile past the junction, you soon emerge onto the broad sandy beach just north of Heceta Head.

10

Kentucky Falls

Location: Siuslaw National Forest

Distance (round-trip): 4¼ miles

Time (round-trip): 3½ hours

Vertical rise: 750 feet

Difficulty: moderate

Maps: USGS 7½' Mercer Lake; USFS Siuslaw National Forest

Best season: spring, summer, fall

This moderate hike takes you into the heart of Oregon's coastal rain forest and provides you with views of three incredible waterfalls.

Getting There

From Eugene follow US 126 for 33 miles west to the WHITAKER CREEK RECREATION AREA sign and turn left. From Florence follow US 126 east 26 miles to the WHITAKER CREEK RECREATION AREA sign and turn right. Follow the road south 1½ miles and turn right across the bridge. Another 1½ miles brings you to Dunn Ridge Road. Turn left and follow the road for 7 miles to Knowles Creek Road. Turn left onto the gravel Knowles Creek Road and follow it 2¾ miles, past the recent logging activities, to Forest Service Road 23. Turn right and follow the road 1½ miles to Forest Service Road 2300-919. Turn right again and follow for 2¾ miles the paved Forest Service Road 2300-919 to the trailhead parking area on the right.

Although the drive to the trailhead is long, windy, and an exercise in trust, it also offers some amazing views, especially along Dunn Ridge. Looking east over the countless ridges of the Coast Range and Cascade foothills are the snow-tipped Cascade peaks of the Three Sisters and Mount Bachelor.

Special Notes

There are several steep drop-offs along the trail and care should be taken when hiking with small children. No permits or access fees are required.

Coast and Coast Range

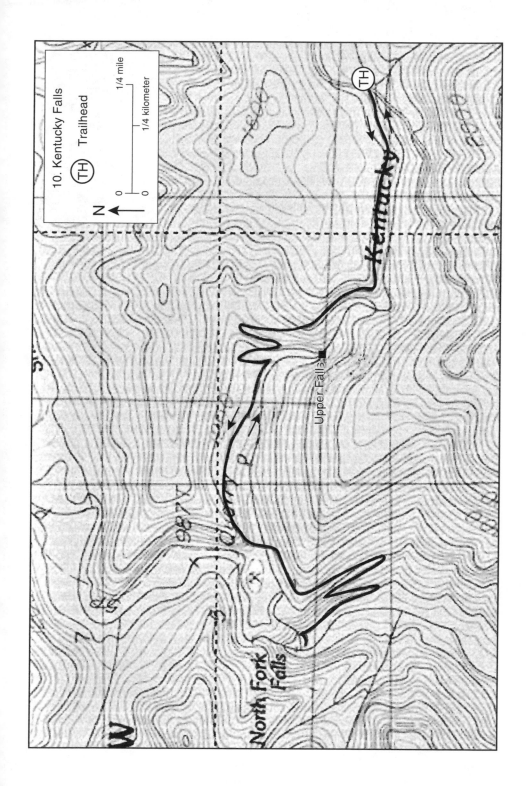

10. Kentucky Falls

TH Trailhead

N

1/4 mile

1/4 kilometer

0

0

Kentucky

Upper Falls

North Fork Falls

Upper Kentucky Falls

The Trail

Tumbling over a 15-million-year-old basalt cliff that was once part of the Pacific Ocean floor are some of the most scenic waterfalls in the Coast Range. The trail's location is far enough inland to be sheltered from the millions of tourists who visit the Oregon coast each year.

The trailhead is located on the left, just up the road from the parking area. The trail begins along Kentucky Creek, through moss-covered, old-growth Douglas fir and hemlock. Some of these ancient trees are more than 8 feet in diameter and 300 feet high. As you walk along the trail, the creek slowly begins to drop away. After ¾ mile the trail breaks out of the forest onto the cliff just above Upper Kentucky Falls. The trail, which is cut into the basalt cliff, then begins a series of switchbacks, each with its own unique views, that carry you down to the base of the 90-foot-tall, tiered waterfall.

Continuing along the trail, you pass several scenic rapids and cascades before you gradually lose sight of Kentucky Creek, although it is always within earshot. From here the trail reenters the forest where you soon encounter a short log bridge crossing a small seasonal creek. A little more than ¼ mile brings you to a second, larger, log footbridge spanning Kentucky Creek. The trail soon crests the rim of the river valley where you begin another series of long gentle switchbacks that lead you ¾ mile down to the Smith River and the wooden observation platform for the Lower Kentucky Falls.

The single-tiered, 100-foot-high falls is tucked away in a dell surrounded by moss-covered fir and alder. Just to the left of Lower Kentucky Falls and cascading over the same basalt cliff is the 100-foot fan of North Fork Falls on the North Fork of the Smith River. The flight of stairs off the observation platform joins a short path leading to a small bench just above the confluence of Kentucky Creek and the Smith River and offers the best view of the unique twin waterfalls and a great place to picnic. Sunrise or sunset is the best time to photograph the falls; make sure you bring along a wide-angle lens to capture both falls. If you decide to scramble down to the water's edge, watch for the broad-leafed and very thorny devil's club, which grows all along the creek.

The return trip is all uphill, so take some time to rest and watch the American dippers as they dart among the rocks and under the water near Upper Kentucky Falls. Also watch for Roosevelt elk and deer, which are numerous in the area.

In addition to the fir and hemlock, early spring brings trilliums, shootingstars, monkeyflowers, and a few rhododendrons. In August, you may be able to find a handful of salmonberries for an extra boost of energy on the way back.

11

Blacklock Point

Location: Floras Lake State Park

Distance (round-trip): 6¾ miles

Time (round-trip): 4½ hours

Vertical rise: 200 feet

Difficulty: moderate

Map: USGS 7½' Floras Lake, Cape Blanco

Best season: spring, summer, fall

Often overshadowed by Cape Blanco, the western-most point in the lower United States, Blacklock Point offers a unique coastal landscape of 300-foot-high sandstone cliffs plunging straight into the Pacific.

Getting There

From Port Orford follow US 101 north 7 miles to the airport sign pointing left. Turn left onto County Road 160 and follow it 2¾ miles, past the cranberry bogs, to the road's end at the airport entrance. The trailhead is located at the gate to the left.

Special Notes

Several steep drop-offs exist along Blacklock Point and care should be taken when hiking with small children. Extreme care must be taken when hiking near the sandstone cliffs. This portion of the trail is not recommended for children. No permits or access fees are required.

The Trail

Unlike many of the headlands to the north, Blacklock Point and Cape Blanco are not composed of Columbia River Basalt. They are much older, dating back 100 to 200 million years, and are composed of sediments from the sea floor. The sediments were then transformed and lifted by continental forces, as the Pacific Plate slid under the North American plate just offshore. This uplift continues today at a rate of nearly 3 inches per 100 years.

The trail begins at the gate on the left, marking the border of the undeveloped state

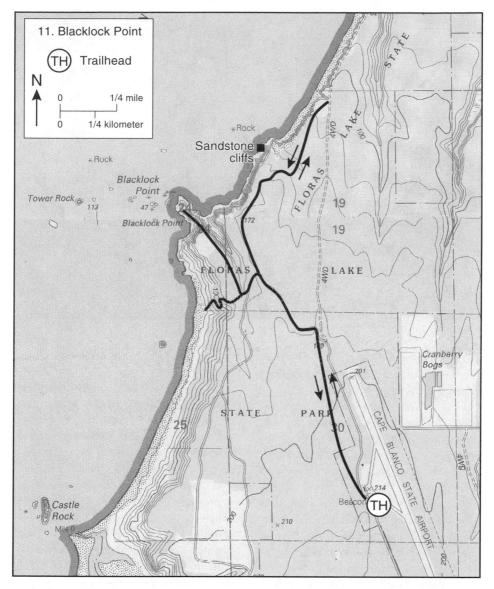

11. Blacklock Point

(TH) Trailhead

N

| 0 | 1/4 mile |
| 0 | 1/4 kilometer |

*Rock

Sandstone cliffs

*Rock

Blacklock Point

Tower Rock 113

Blacklock Point

47

172

FLORAS

19

19

FLORAS LAKE

Cranberry Bogs

STATE PARK

25

30

201

CAPE BLANCO STATE AIRPORT

214

Beacon (TH)

Castle Rock

Mile 0

210

---

park, and follows an old dirt service road alongside the airport. After a ¾-mile stroll through salal and spruce, you cross a small seasonal creek, which is shortly followed by a trail junction. Stay to the left where you join the Oregon Coast Trail. Ignore the various side trails and follow the Blacklock Point markers to the left at the next junction.

Continue on as the trail cuts through the dense growth of salal. Spring also brings the pink and white flowers of rhododendron that are abundant along the trail.

After ½ mile you arrive at yet another junction. Again follow the markers to the left where, after a few hundred yards, you will encounter still another fork. Take a right here,

Sandstone Cliffs from Blacklock Point

and in a little more than a ¼ mile, you break into the grassy meadows of Blacklock Point followed by the rocky cliffs just beyond.

Looking south from the cliffs edge provides a beautiful view of Castle Rock sitting just offshore from the mouth of the Sixes River, Cape Blanco, and the Cape Blanco lighthouse. The lighthouse was completed in 1870 and is Oregon's oldest continuously operating light. It is also Oregon's highest, standing 256 feet above the sea, and in 1903, home to Oregon's first woman keeper, Mable E. Bretherton. Unlike the rotating light you see today, the original first-order Fresnel lens was fixed to shine a solid beam of light out to sea marking the westernmost point in the lower United States. Visitors are welcome daily from April through October and the hours of 10 AM to 3:30 PM.

Blacklock Point is also home to a relatively undeveloped archaeological site of an ancient shell midden that dates back 7,500 years.

For those wishing to walk along the beach, do not attempt to hike down the point but instead follow the trail back to the first junction and turn right. A short ½-mile trail leads to the beach where a 1-mile stroll brings you to the mouth of the Sixes River.

To reach the sandstone cliffs, turn left at the first fork on your return from the point and then left again at the fork following a few hundred yards. You will once again pass through a dense growth of salal before the spruce forest takes over. After ½ mile, the trail once again rejoins the bluff. As you continue, a maze of short trails to the left lead through the salal undergrowth to various cliff-edge views. After investigating the views, continue along the main trail, where after another ½ mile you come to a short wooden footbridge crossing a small creek. A few hundred yards past the bridge, a series of trails break through the dense growth of salal and onto the sandstone bluffs. Here the rain and wind have created countless sculptures in the soft sandstone. A few yards farther bring you to the edge of the 300-foot-high cliffs and perhaps to some of the most unique scenery on the coast. A few yards south, the small stream carves through the sandstone and plunges 150 feet onto the beach below.

From here, the trail continues on another 2 miles to the beach and Floras Lake. However, to complete the moderate, 6¾-mile hike, backtrack your route.

II

Columbia River Gorge

Multonomah Falls Bridge

A little more than 10,000 years ago, during the last Ice Age, an ice dam formed an immense lake in the region around Missoula, Montana. As the waters behind the dam deepened, the ice dam failed. The resulting deluge raced across eastern Washington, scouring the landscape clean and inundating the Columbia River. As the floodwaters entered the gorge, they deepened, increased velocity, and carved away at the edges of the gorge. At their height, the floodwaters would have submerged the city of Portland under 200 feet of water. The waters then filled the Willamette Valley, creating a temporary inland sea. This scenario was repeated as many as 100 times and is responsible for creating the steep cliffs that the spectacular waterfalls of the Columbia River Gorge now cascade over.

A stone's throw away from Portland, a city with a population of a little more than 1 million in the metropolitan area, the short trails around the signature falls, such as Multnomah Falls, can become very crowded during summer weekends. However, the majority of these people rarely venture more than a mile or two up the longer trails, and during the off-season many of the trails are nearly empty.

Climate

The Columbia River Gorge has a surprisingly wide variation in climate. From the lush green forest surrounding Multnomah Falls to the semiarid prairie grasslands of Rowena Crest, it is less than 60 miles. When the temperatures reach the 80s in Portland, they often approach 100 degrees in the town of The Dalles. Much of this disparity in climate has to do with the Cascade Mountains. As the cool, moisture-rich air encounters the high Cascade Range, it rises up and releases its moisture on the west side in the form of rain or a heavy mist. The gorge also

has another effect that has endeared the region to windsurfers around the world. As low-pressure systems make their way up the Pacific Coast, it draws the usually higher pressure air of the east, funneling it down the gorge and generating winds that often reach 40 to 50 miles per hour.

Similar to the Coast Range, the majority of precipitation occurs during the winter months, leaving the summer months relatively dry. While temperatures are typically moderate throughout the year, the Columbia River Gorge does experience two or three weeks of freezing temperatures during the winter, often accompanied by snow. Winter temperatures on the west side of the gorge range in the 40s and 50s, and summer temperatures are typically in the 70s or 80s. Temperatures on the east side of the gorge are a little more extreme, ranging from 5 to 10 degrees cooler in winter and 5 to 10 degrees warmer in the summer.

Precautions

Many of the trails in the gorge pass by steep cliffs and rushing white-water streams. In many instances, the edge can be unstable or slippery, even when it is not raining. Stay on the trails in these areas and refrain from climbing over fences and railings.

Although the gorge is located less than an hour away from Portland, it is a true wilderness area, and it's easy to become turned around and disoriented by the often-unmarked trail forks on the longer hikes. Make sure to carry a map and compass when hiking the longer trails in the region.

Attractions

Located 4 miles west of Cascade Locks, the Bonneville Dam Visitor Center offers exhibits and interpretive displays about the building of the dam and the geology, cultural, and natural history of the gorge. Also located at the dam is Oregon's oldest fish hatchery. At the Bonneville Fish Hatchery, you can peer into the rearing ponds to see thousands of salmon smolt (young, immature salmon less than 6 months old); other ponds contain huge rainbow trout. Vending machines dispense a handful of fish food for 25¢, allowing you to feed the already chubby fish. A separate pond provides an underwater view of the prehistoric white sturgeon. These immense fish, the largest in North America, can reach lengths of 19 feet, weigh more than 1,800 pounds, and reach an age of more than 100 years.

The Columbia Gorge Discovery Center is located on the west end of The Dalles. The center houses interactive displays that tell the story of the volcanic upheavals and raging floods that created the gorge. Additional exhibits explore the diversity of plant life and wildlife and the ancient lives of early Native Americans who called the gorge home.

Sauvie Island is located just 10 miles west of Portland on US 30 and in the spring and fall offers some of the best birding opportunities in the area as it serves as a primary stop for migrating birds. Sandhill cranes, egrets, heron, coots, grebes, swans, geese, eagles, and numerous ducks and songbirds are common during migration periods. The island also provides a well-developed network of hiking trails as well as canoe paths. In addition, the island is an extremely productive agricultural area and offers an abundance of fresh fruit and vegetables during the summer and well into the fall.

12

Sauvie Island—Warrior Rock

Location: 22 miles northwest of Portland

Distance (round-trip): 7 miles

Time (round-trip): 4½ hours

Vertical gain: none

Difficulty: easy

Maps: USGS 7½' St. Helens; Sauvie Island Refuge Trail Guide

Best season: spring, summer, fall, winter

Sauvie Island is a local mecca for bird-watchers. An abundance of migratory birds, such as ducks, geese, swans, egrets, and sandhill cranes, populate the island in the fall, winter, and spring. Nesting bald eagles can be seen in late winter and early spring. Heron, hawks, and osprey also call the refuge home and can be seen year-round.

Getting There
From Portland, travel west 10 miles on US 30. At the sign for the refuge, turn right over the Sauvie Island Bridge and onto NW Sauvie Island Road. Follow NW Sauvie Island Road 1¾ miles north and turn right onto Reeder Road. Follow Reeder Road 12½ miles to the parking area where the road ends.

Special Notes
Bring your binoculars or small spotting scope for bird-watching. During the spring and summer, mosquitoes are abundant and repellent is a necessity. A Sauvie Island Wildlife Refuge parking permit is required to park at the trailhead and is available at many private vendors ($3 daily, $10.50 annually).

The Trail
The ancestral winter home of the Multnomah Indians, Sauvie Island has long been a site of human activity. Arrowheads, fishing points, and other stone tools can still be found at old campsites along the Columbia River and Multnomah Channel.

In 1792 Lt. William Broughton, from Captain George Vancouver's expedition to find the mythical Northwest Passage between the Atlantic and Pacific Oceans, set out to explore the island. Upon landing on the island, Broughton was immediately surrounded by 23 Chinook war canoes. After hastily making peace with the Chinooks, he called the place "Warrior Rock."

In 1805 Lewis and Clark made note of the island on their way to the Pacific. They estimated the island's Native American population, living among five villages, to be about 800. On their return voyage in 1806, the Corps of Discovery camped just across the Columbia and traded with the Multnomah for fish and *wapato,* a local potato-like root. Wapato was so abundant on the island that the Corps christened it Wapato Island. By the 1830s diseases such as smallpox and malaria had decimated the native population. Dairy farms were started on the island to supply nearby Fort Vancouver. A French Canadian employee of the Hudson Bay Company, Laurent Sauve, oversaw the farms and became the island's namesake.

Begin the hike by climbing over the parking lot fence stile. After a short walk through a pasture, the trail then turns into a dirt service road that parallels the Columbia River's shoreline. After hiking ½ mile through cottonwoods and a few scrub oak, Henrici Lake appears on the left. Several short trails lead to the water's edge and offer an opportunity to view the numerous migratory birds that stop at the island on their trip north or south, depending on the season, of course. Sandhill cranes, Canada geese, egrets, and swans can all be seen at various times of the year. The area also supports several nesting pairs of bald eagles and osprey.

As you continue along the service road through cottonwood and ash trees, you encounter several short trails to the right that lead to sandy beaches along the Columbia.

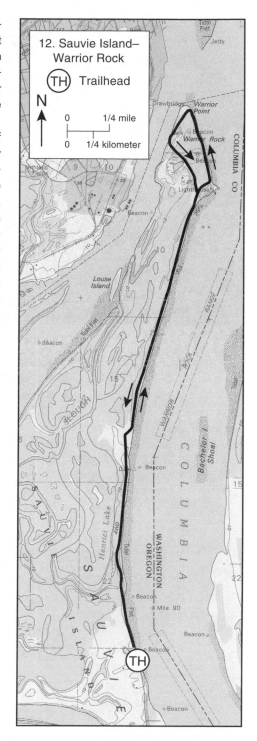

12. Sauvie Island–
Warrior Rock

(TH) Trailhead

N

0   1/4 mile
0   1/4 kilometer

Sauvie Island sunrise

After 2½ miles, the trail opens to a meadow and then forks. Take the right fork ¼ mile to the Warrior Rock lighthouse perched on a small basalt rock outcropping. The 28-foot-tall tower seen today was built in the 1930s; the original two-story structure was built in 1889, with the single-room first floor serving as the keeper's quarters. While the lighthouse is off limits, a beautiful little sand beach lies just to the left and makes for a great place to picnic. Back on the trail, follow the left fork to a viewpoint of the St. Helens courthouse, marina, and replica of the original lighthouse. The return trip follows the same service road back to the parking lot.

13

Angels Rest

Location: Columbia River Gorge National Scenic Area

Distance (round-trip): 4½ miles

Time (round-trip): 3 hours

Vertical gain: 1,400 feet

Difficulty: moderate

Maps: USGS 7½' Bridal Veil, Multnomah Falls; USFS Trails of the Columbia Gorge

Best season: spring, summer, fall, winter

This ancient basalt dike protrudes into the Columbia River Gorge and, at 1,500 feet above the river, offers spectacular views up and down the gorge. From this vista you can imagine the series of immense floods, the largest ever recorded, that helped carve the gorge some 15,000 years ago during the last Ice Age.

Getting There

From Portland travel east 28 miles on I-84 and take exit 28 (Bridal Veil). Follow the road for ¼ mile to the junction of the Columbia River Scenic Highway and the parking lot for the Angels Rest Trail. From Hood River travel west 26 miles on I-84 to exit 35 and turn left onto the Columbia River Scenic Highway. Follow the scenic highway 7½ miles to the Angels Rest trailhead and parking lot.

Special Notes

Due to its proximity to Portland, the trails of the Columbia Gorge can become crowded during the spring and summer. However, most tourists choose to hike the trails around the signature falls such as Multnomah. A Northwest Forest Pass is required to park at the trailhead and is available from many private vendors ($5 daily, $30 annually).

The Trail

The trailhead for this popular trail is well marked and begins at the eastern end of the parking lot across the Columbia Gorge Scenic Highway. The first portion of the trail climbs through a typical second-growth

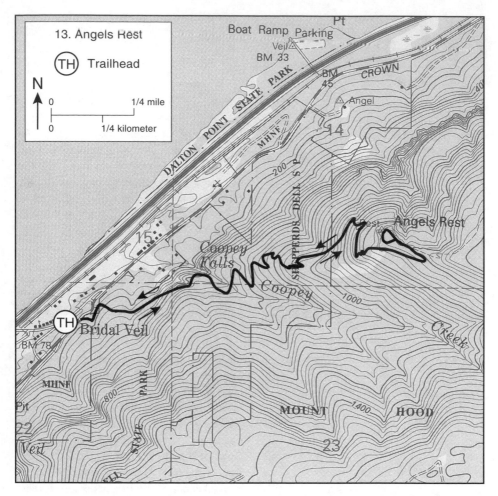

Douglas fir forest with a moderately thick undergrowth of vine maple and sword and bracken fern. Poison oak is also abundant along the trail, so take extra care if you decide to step off the path. The trail soon joins the ridgeline created by Coopey Creek, and after ½ mile you get your first glimpse of the 100-foot-high Coopey Falls. A few white trillium can be found in early spring followed later in the year by larkspur and wild Oregon iris.

The trail passes by another small cascade immediately before a small footbridge spanning Coopey Creek just above the falls and a little more than ½ mile from the trailhead. From here the trail steepens and climbs through several long switchbacks as it moves away from the creek and climbs up the ridge. After about another ½ mile the trail begins to open up as it passes through the site of a forest fire that roared through the area in 1991. The trail works its way through a small scree field (an accumulation of rocky debris) below the bluff and then up to the ridge crest where the trail forks. The right fork continues on to join the Columbia River Gorge Trail system where another 4½ miles brings you to Wahkeena Falls, or after

Angels Rest view

3 miles it brings you to Devils Rest. Take the left fork, which follows the rocky ridgeline a few hundred feet to the flat, basalt bluff of Angels Rest.

The roughly marked trail on top of the bluff makes a short loop around the perimeter. The bluff is covered in a thick growth of vine maple, with numerous "unofficial" trails cutting back and forth. Along the edge spectacular views up and down the river include Beacon Rock, Crown Point, and Roster Rock.

14

Triple Falls

Location: Columbia River Scenic Highway, 34 miles east of Portland, Columbia River Gorge National Scenic Area

Distance (round-trip): 4½ miles

Time (round-trip): 3 hours

Vertical gain: 700 feet

Difficulty: moderate

Maps: USGS 7½' Bridal Veil Multnomah Falls; USFS Trails of the Columbia Gorge

Best season: spring, summer, fall, winter

One of the gems in the Columbia River Gorge Trail system, the Triple Falls Trail offers spectacular vistas of the Columbia River, passes behind a waterfall, and peers into a hidden, moss-covered gorge.

Getting There

From Portland drive 35 miles east on I-84 to exit 35 (Ainsworth State Park). Follow the Columbia River Scenic Highway 1½ miles to the Horsetail Falls Trail parking area on the right. From Hood River take exit 35 (Ainsworth State Park) and follow the Columbia River Scenic Highway 1½ miles to Horsetail Falls.

Special Notes

While the lower portions of the trail can be busy during spring and summer weekends, the section along Oneonta Gorge and Triple Falls is usually much less populated. The low-water levels of the summer and early fall months provide the only opportunity to hike into Oneonta Gorge.

The Trail

The trail begins just east of Horsetail Falls at the Ponytail Falls trailhead. After climbing ¼ mile through several switchbacks, the trail rounds the bluff where Ponytail Falls seems to leap from the basalt bluff. The trail continues behind the 80-foot single plunge of the falls along a shallow cave created by the falls's old splash pool, which washed away the softer sediment buried underneath one of the many lava flows of the area.

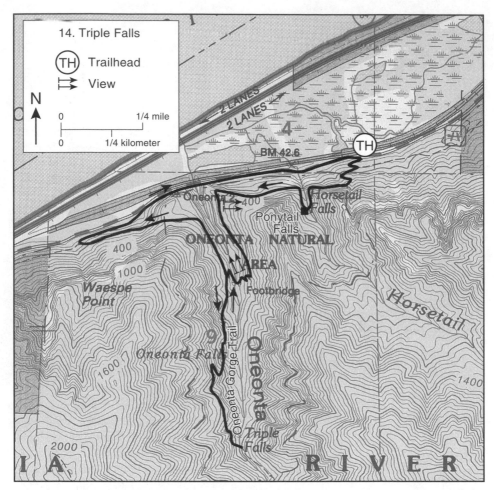

Another ½ mile through cedar, Douglas fir, and vine maple brings you to a fork; stay to the right where an unmaintained trail brings you to a basalt outcropping offering a spectacular view up and down the Columbia River Gorge. After another 100 yards, you rejoin the main trail. As you continue along the trail, follow the rim of Oneonta Gorge where, after ½ mile, the trail switchbacks down Oneonta Gorge and to the bridge looking onto the 60-foot-high Oneonta Falls. On the second switchback down to the bridge, you pass a great view looking downstream into the Oneonta Gorge. From the bridge, a short climb of a few hundred feet brings you to the junction with the Oneonta Gorge Trail. Turn left and follow the trail a steep, sometimes precarious ¾ mile to the scenic Triple Falls viewpoint located on a short trail spur to the left.

The best view of Triple Falls is from this cliff-edge viewpoint. From here the three chutes of the 130-foot-high falls are framed by the maple trees that overhang the creek following the main trail. Another ¼ mile brings you to the bridge crossing the creek

Triple Falls from the viewpoint

just above the falls. This is a good place to stop, rest, and have lunch.

On your return trip you can either backtrack down Ponytail Falls Trail or take the Oneonta Gorge Trail back to the Columbia River Scenic Highway where, after ½ mile, it leads you back to the Horsetail Falls parking area. It's roughly the same distance for either route you chose.

In summer, you may want to put on some shorts and sandals and hike into Oneonta Gorge. The cold, clear water of the creek covers the floor wall to wall but never gets more than waist deep. Branches of fir and cedar trees form a natural canopy over the rounded moss- and fern-covered walls. After approximately ½ mile, you come to a little-known and rarely visited 100-foot falls.

15

Wahkeena Falls to Multnomah Falls

Location: Columbia River Scenic Highway, 31 miles east of Portland, Columbia River Gorge National Scenic Area

Distance (round-trip): 5¼ miles, 2¾ miles (Perdition Trail)

Time (round-trip): 5 hours, 3 hours

Vertical gain: 2,300 feet, 1,200 feet

Difficulty: moderate

Maps: USGS 7½' Bridal Veil, Multnomah Falls; USFS Trails of the Columbia Gorge

Best season: spring, summer, fall, winter

Multnomah Falls is the scenic attraction most visited in the state of Oregon. On average, 1½ million people visit the falls each year. In contrast, Crater Lake National Park attracts only 500,000. However, the vast majority of these visitors stay near the gift shop or only hike the lower portion of the trail, leaving the upper section to Wahkeena Falls relatively unpopulated.

Getting There

From Portland drive 28 miles east on I-84 to exit 28 (Bridal Veil). Follow the Columbia River Scenic Highway east 2¾ miles to the Wahkeena Falls Trail parking area on the right. From Hood River take exit 35 (Bridal Veil) and follow the Columbia River Scenic Highway 5 miles to Wahkeena Falls.

Special Notes

Tremendously popular, there is no way to avoid the crowds around Multnomah Falls. However, if you'd like to experience a unique conclusion to your hike, the facilities in the historic lodge include a coffee stand and a great little restaurant specializing in Northwest dishes, such as fresh smoked salmon, sturgeon, or halibut. After your hike, you can enjoy a latte or a fresh salmon dinner. No fees or permits are required.

The Trail

The trailhead is located at the west end of the Wahkeena Falls parking area. The trail begins by climbing ¼ mile through the typical gorge undergrowth of vine maple, sword fern, Douglas fir, and occasional western red cedar before coming to the scenic

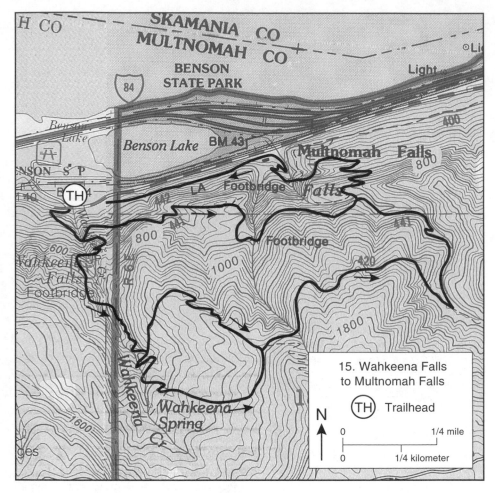

15. Wahkeena Falls
to Multnomah Falls

(TH) Trailhead

N

0   1/4 mile

0   1/4 kilometer

moss-covered stone footbridge at the base of the falls. The falls itself is a series of smaller cascades tumbling through a winding chute for a total of 240 feet. At ½ mile from the trailhead mark you will need to make a choice to either stay to the right and continue along Wahkeena Creek or turn left and take the shorter Perdition Trail.

Continuing the climb along the Wahkeena Trail after ½ mile you come to two short spurs, one to the right and one to the left, that lead to Lemon's and Monument viewpoints. Back on the main trail, you soon rejoin and cross the creek twice on your

way up the canyon to the 50-foot-high fan of Fairy Falls, which is roughly 1¼ miles from the parking area.

A few hundred feet further will bring you to the lower junction of the Vista Point Trail, the first of several junctions. Stay right and in a little more than ¼ mile you arrive at the Angels Rest Trail junction. Turn left. After another ¼ mile you come to two more junctions; stay to your right at the first (upper junction of the Vista Point Trail) and left at the second (Devils Rest Trail).

From here, the upper portion of the trail levels off and provides glimpses of the

Columbia River 1,500 feet below (you are now on a very steep clearing on the hillside). In the spring, wildflowers are abundant along various sections of the trail. Trillium, glacier lilies, and blue camas bloom in the early spring and are followed by columbine, candy flower, bleeding heart, foxglove, and tiger lily.

After 1 mile you arrive at Multnomah Creek and the junction of the Larch Mountain Trail. Turn left and from here it's all downhill. Follow the trail along the creek for ¾ mile to the brink of Multnomah Falls. Along the way you follow the tumbling creek past Dutchman Tunnel and several smaller scenic cascades.

Multnomah is a two-tiered falls totaling 621 feet in height, which easily makes it the state's highest waterfall and the second highest in the nation. The first section is 542 feet high, and the second section, which passes under the signature stone bridge, is 60 feet high. From the upper viewpoint of Multnomah Falls, it's a relatively steep descent along a paved trail for the next mile to the historic Multnomah Falls Lodge. Take your time on the way down, not only to absorb the power and beauty of the falls, but also look closely at the cliff behind the falls, which is composed of six separate flows of Columbia River basalt that date from 6 to 15 million years ago.

For those short on time or looking for a shorter, less strenuous hike, you may want to take Perdition Trail. It begins ¼ mile past the Wahkeena Falls bridge and, after 1¼ miles, ends a few hundred yards above the upper viewpoint on the Larch Mountain Trail. Although not as scenic as the upper trail, on this trail you pass several viewpoints

Foxglove, a common wildflower in Oregon

that offer great views of the Columbia River and the surrounding gorge. The return route for both trails is a ¾-mile return path back to Wahkeena Falls, which parallels the old Columbia River Scenic Highway, begins at the far west end of the Multnomah Falls parking area.

The falls and the surrounding 300 acres were originally owned by Simon Benson, who, in 1914, commissioned Italian stonemasons to construct the bridge between the upper and lower falls. In 1915 he donated the land to the City of Portland. In 1925 the City of Portland built the lodge, which contains every type of rock found in the gorge, at the then-exorbitant cost of $40,000. The lodge has been listed on the National Register of Historic Places since 1981.

16

Wahclella Falls

Location: Exit 40 off I-84 near the Bonneville Dam, 40 miles east of Portland, 20 miles west of Hood River

Distance (round-trip): 1¾ miles

Time (round-trip): 1 hour

Vertical gain: 300 feet

Difficulty: easy

Maps: USGS 7½' Bonneville Dam, Tanner Butte; USFS Trails of the Columbia Gorge

Best season: spring, summer, fall, winter

The cool air and refreshing mist near the falls plunge pool make this a nice short hike on hot summer days. However, during times of high runoff this 350-foot-tall, two-tiered falls can be a thunderous experience as water from the upper tier funnels into a small slot and is pushed out for the final 60-foot plunge.

Getting There

From Portland travel east 40 miles on I-84 and take exit 40 (Bonneville Dam). Turn right (opposite the dam) and follow the road along Tanner Creek for a few hundred feet to the parking lot. From Hood River travel west 20 miles on I-84 to exit 40, turn left under I-84 and follow the road along Tanner Creek for a few hundred feet to the parking lot.

Special Notes

The trail and adjacent Bonneville Dam make for a great family outing. The manicured grounds at the Bonneville Fish Hatchery have a nice picnic area, and the hatchery offers self-guided tours of the salmon incubators and rearing ponds. Water from Tanner Creek is diverted into several ponds where you can feed large rainbow trout and view 10-foot-long, 600-pound white sturgeon. A Northwest Forest Pass is required to park at the trailhead and is available from many private vendors ($5 daily, $30 annually).

The Trail

The trail begins by following Tanner Creek along a gravel service road ¼ mile to a

Wahclella Falls and trail bridge

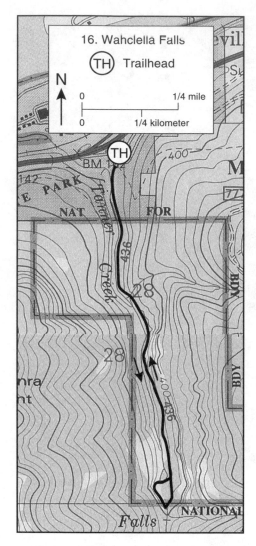

The trail continues through big leaf maple and Douglas fir along the creek where you are almost certain to get a glimpse of American dippers feeding in the swift waters of the creek. Although somewhat rare, the elusive harlequin duck may be sighted during the spring and early summer. During much of the year harlequins are found along the coast on offshore sea stacks or in bays and estuaries. However, during the breeding season they nest on rocks or fallen trees along mountain streams. Their feeding habits are similar to that of the dipper, diving to the bottom and walking along the bottom by holding onto rocks in search of aquatic food.

Continuing along the main trail for another ¾ mile you arrive at a junction. Follow the upper left trail where, after another ¼ mile, you come to the plunge pool of Wachlella Falls. The 120-foot-high falls is two tiered, with the difficult-to-view top section plunging into a narrow slot and small pool, which then spills out for the final 60-foot drop.

Just below the plunge pool the trail continues across a footbridge to the other side of the creek and under a deep overhang of the surrounding basalt cliffs. In 1973 this was the sight of a landslide that brought down the rubble and house-sized boulders you'll see on this side of the creek. Just one look at the older boulders in the stream and the steep basalt cliffs tell you that this was not the first slide nor is it the last. From the footbridge the trail continues for another few hundred yards where it again crosses Tanner Creek on a newly built footbridge and rejoins the trail at the previous fork.

small diversion dam for the Bonneville Fish Hatchery. From here the trail crosses a small footbridge that passes below a small seasonal cascade, which can be quite spectacular, and wet, with a heavy runoff.

17

Eagle Creek

Location: 41 miles east of Portland, Columbia River Gorge National Scenic Area

Distance (round-trip): 12½ miles

Time (round-trip): 9 hours

Vertical gain: 1,200 feet

Difficulty: difficult

Maps: USGS 7½' Bonneville Dam, Tanner Butte, Wahtum Lake; USFS Trails of the Columbia Gorge

Best season: spring, summer, fall, winter

Built in the 1910s to compliment the then-new Columbia River Highway, Eagle Creek is one of the most spectacular trails in the entire Northwest. The trail is precariously cut into the basalt cliffs high above the creek and passes six major waterfalls.

Getting There
From Portland travel east 41 miles on I-84 to exit 41 (Eagle Creek). Turn right at the hatchery building and follow Eagle Creek Road ½ mile to the trailhead. As there is no westbound exit from Hood River, take exit 40 (Bonneville Dam) and double back on I-84 to the Eagle Creek exit.

Special Notes
Located only 40 minutes from Portland, this trail is extremely busy during the spring and summer months. This trail is not recommended for young children due to the trail's path along numerous cliffs. A Northwest Forest Pass is required to park at the trailhead and is available at most ranger stations and from many private vendors ($5 daily, $30 annually).

The Trail
The trailhead is located at the south end of the parking area beside Eagle Creek. The trail begins by following the creek through western cedar, Douglas fir, and big leaf maple. Soon you begin climbing up the moss-covered basalt canyon walls. After ¾ mile you reach the first of several cliffs to be traversed. A cable handrail is mounted on the inside cliff wall and provides some sense

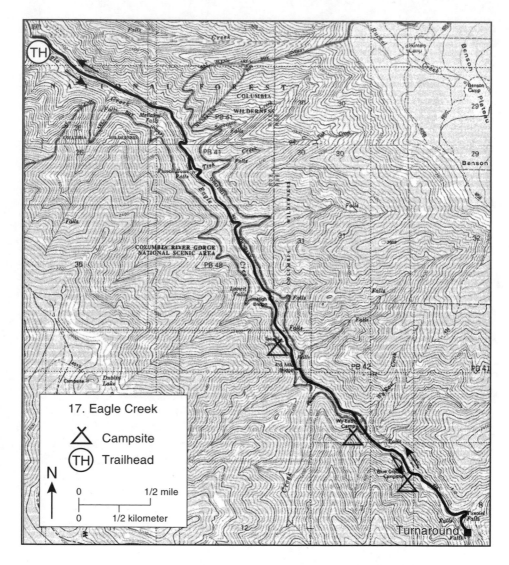

17. Eagle Creek

⚠️ Campsite

(TH) Trailhead

N

| 0 | 1/2 mile |
| 0 | 1/2 kilometer |

Turnaround

of security. Another ¾ mile brings you to a junction with a short trail spur that leads to the viewpoint for 100-foot-high Metlako Falls, the first of the five major falls along the trail. The view of the falls is best during the winter months when the trees are bare. However, spring and summer vegetation provide an almost fairy-tale appearance.

Continuing along the main trail for another ¼ mile you reach the junction for Punchbowl Falls. The main trail continues to the left, while to the right a short trail spur leads ¼ mile to a rocky beach just downstream from the falls. This view of the 30-foot falls is the best known and certainly the most photographed. Although the view is still very photogenic, a large Douglas fir has fallen into the narrow gorge of the splash pool and partially obstructed the view for the past several years. The stone beach is a

Punchbowl Falls

nice place to have a picnic, rest your feet in the cold water, or just sit and watch the swallows and American dippers.

Another ¼ mile along the main trail brings you to the Punchbowl Falls Overlook, which provides a beautiful view looking down onto the falls and "punchbowl."

From here the trail climbs slightly through old-growth fir and cedar. After a mile you come to the most nerve-racking portion of the trail as it passes along the Eagle Creek Gorge and on to High Bridge, which crosses the gorge. Here the trail is carved along the side of the gorge, 120 feet above the roaring waters below. Hold onto the cable handrail and look across the gorge for Loowit Falls as it cascades into Eagle Creek.

One-quarter mile past High Bridge you come to the broad, 50-foot-high Skook-nichuk Falls. A short trail spur on the right leads to Tenas Camp. From here the trail is at creek level for another ¾ mile where you cross the creek on a footbridge bringing you to the Wy'East Backpacking Camp. At the 5-mile mark, the trail again forks; the left fork leads to the Benson Plateau and the Pacific Crest Trail after 3 steep miles. If you are plan-ning on camping, take the right fork to the third camping area, Blue Grouse Campsite, just ¼ mile away. It's best to arrive on a weekday or very early at any of the camping areas. Camping is only allowed in the desig-nated areas, and with the limited space they fill up quickly during the summer months. Also note that open campfires are strongly discouraged. Check at the Eagle Creek ranger station for any additional regulations.

From here the trail once again begins to climb the walls of the canyon. After ¾ mile you come to the 120-foot-tall Tunnel Falls. Here the trail leads up to and behind the falls through a tunnel carved into the basalt. It's a truly singular experience to pass be-hind the falls and emerge so close to the falling water while perched on the rocky ledge almost 100 feet in the air. A few hun-dred yards more brings you to the top of Eagle Creek Falls.

On your return trip, take some time to look for trillium, monkeyflower, wild iris, and the occasional avalanche lily. Wild straw-berries can also be found on some of the sunny slopes. Look for hawks and bald ea-gles as they soar above the canyon or perch in trees overlooking the water.

18

Tom McCall Nature Preserve

Location: Columbia River Scenic Highway, 76 miles east of Portland, Columbia River Gorge National Scenic Area

Distance (round-trip): 5½ miles

Time (round-trip): 4 hours

Vertical gain: 1,400 feet

Difficulty: moderate

Map: USGS 7½' White Salmon

Best season: spring, summer, fall, winter

In stark contrast to the lush trails of the western side of the Columbia River Gorge, the east end is a stark, dry land of scrub oak, sagebrush, grasslands, and basalt plateaus. The nature preserves land is owned by The Nature Conservancy, a non-profit organization that purchases sensitive lands and sets them aside for restoration and preservation.

Getting There
From Portland drive 68 miles east on I-84 to exit 69 (Mosier). Follow the Columbia River Scenic Highway east 6½ miles to the Rowena Crest viewpoint. From The Dalles travel west on I-84 to exit 76 (Rowena) and follow the Columbia River Scenic Highway 5 miles to the Rowena Crest viewpoint.

Special Notes
The wildflowers along the lower ponds make this an excellent early spring to early summer hike. Midsummer temperatures often reach into the upper 90s, making the trip to Tom McCall Point a bit of an effort. If you do plan on hiking in the summer months, be sure to bring extra water. No fees or permits are required, although a donation is suggested at the trailhead.

The Trail
The trail is named after former Oregon governor Tom McCall, who is probably best remembered for encouraging people to visit the state but not stay. However, Governor McCall's accomplishments also include cleaning up the Willamette River, introducing

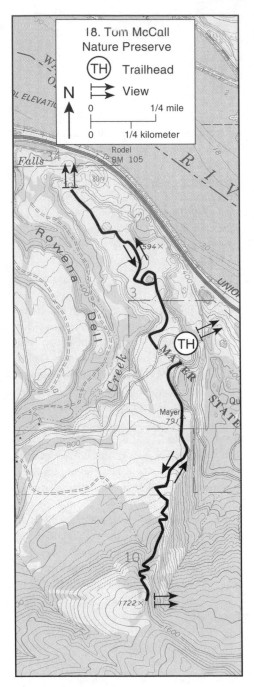

the bottle bill, and protecting Oregon's beaches from private development.

The wildflower season begins in early March and continues through July. Prairie star, shootingstar, and balsamroot thrive. In addition, Thompson's lupine, Columbia parsley, Thompson's waterleaf, and Hood River milk vetch are several species you're likely to see on the preserve and are unique to the Columbia River Gorge.

The Plateau Trail is the best place on the preserve to observe wildflowers. It begins just across the Columbia River Gorge Scenic Highway from the viewpoint entrance. A little more than ¼ mile after you cross the fence stile at the trailhead, you come to the first of two small, cattail-lined ponds. Here a short loop circles the pond. Look and listen for the red-winged blackbirds and Pacific chorus frogs.

Back on the main trail, another ¼ mile brings you to the second and smaller pond where a short trail spur to the right leads to the water's edge. Another 100 yards will bring you to another short spur to the right, which leads to a viewpoint on the basalt cliffs' edge overlooking the Columbia River. The main trail ends only a few hundred yards past the junction with the first viewpoint and offers a sweeping view up and down the Columbia and of the basalt cliffs of the Washington shore. An early morning or late afternoon hike may offer a glimpse of a mule deer or coyote that also frequent the area.

The trail to Tom McCall Point begins at the east side of the Rowena Point parking loop and immediately begins to climb along the basalt rim. The view from the rim looks over the Columbia and the scenic highway's Rowena Curves, one of the most crooked sections of the old road. After a little less than ¼ mile, the trail joins an old service road leading to the left for several yards be-

Rowena Crest and wildflowers

fore turning uphill once again. Another ¼ mile along the exposed rim brings you to a false junction. Stay to the right and follow the steep switchbacks under the power lines. From the power lines, it's another mile of steep switchbacks to reach the top.

Grand, sweeping views of the gorge are offered along the rim, while Indian paintbrush and lupine populate the grasses along the trail. A small grass meadow greets you at the top as do views of Mount Hood, Mount Adams, and the dry eastern end of the Columbia River Gorge.

As little as 10,000 years ago the Missoula floods submerged this landscape under as much as 200 feet of iceberg- and gravel-filled water. As the floodwaters began to recede, immense gravel bars began to form. One of these can be seen on the Washington side of the Columbia, just above the town of Lyle.

III

Cascade Range

Crater Lake Rim from Cleetwood Cove Trail

The Oregon Cascades, the largest geological feature in the state, run from the California border in the south to the Columbia River in the north. This range divides the state into the relatively low, wet western valleys from the high, eastern desert; and the highly populated west from the sparsely populated east.

The Cascades are also a relatively young mountain range with most of the high peaks dating back less than 1 million years. The range is also still quite active. Two other Cascade mountains, Mount Lassen in northern California and Mount St. Helens in southern Washington, erupted in 1915 and 1980, respectively. The recent discovery of a slight uplift occurring just west of the South Sister further illustrates that the range is still active.

The Cascades are home to Oregon's only U.S. National Park, Crater Lake, as well as 20 wilderness areas ranging in size from the largest, Three Sisters, at 285,202 acres, to the smallest, Menagerie, at 5,033 acres. Although thousands of hikers head into the Cascades each year, it is still possible to find areas of solitude because of the region's large size and relatively low population.

Climate

The climate of the Cascades is highly diverse. The western slopes receive nearly 100 inches of precipitation annually, while the eastern slopes may receive as little as 15 inches annually. The lower trails, below 4,000 feet, are usually free of snow from May until October. The upper trails, usually clear by mid-June, are open until September, although snow is possible in the highest elevations year round. Summer temperatures in the higher elevations are typically in the 60s or 70s in the day but can easily drop below freezing at night.

Temperatures in the lower elevations are roughly 5 to 10 degrees warmer.

Precautions

Many of the trails pass by steep cliffs and rushing whitewater. In many instances the edge can be unstable or slippery. Stay on the trails in these areas and refrain from climbing over fences and railings.

When hiking at high elevations, it is important to carry extra water, use sunscreen, and take your time.

Although black bears and mountain lions are abundant in the Cascades, they are very shy and usually avoid contact with humans. However, when camping in the wilderness it is wise to store food away from tents and sleeping areas to keep animals at a distance.

Attractions

Even if you are not a skier, the Timberline Lodge National Historic Landmark is worth visiting. Completed in 1938 by the Federal Works Projects Administration (WPA), it is perched just above the timberline at 6,000 feet and offers spectacular views south to Mount Jefferson. Built entirely by hand, inside and out, by unemployed craftspeople, the lodge contains some truly spectacular iron- and masonry work.

Located at the summit of McKenzie Pass on McKenzie Highway (OR 242) is the Dee Wright Observatory, a stone memorial named for the Civilian Conservation Corps (CCC) foreman who oversaw the highway's construction. Built in the 1930s by the CCC, the observatory offers panoramic views of the Cascade Mountain Range as far north as Mount Hood. A bronze "peak-finder" in the observatory points to the geologic features in the surrounding lava fields.

Just ½ mile past the west entrance to Crater Lake National Park on OR 62 is the

Rogue River Gorge. Here the wild and scenic Rogue River drops into an narrow channel created by a collapsed lava tube. A short trail, complete with interpretive signs, parallels the gorge and offers spectacular views of the churning water below.

The Oregon Caves National Monument is located 20 miles east of Cave Junction on OR 46. Located below some of the largest Douglas fir trees in the state are 3½ miles of marble caverns, the remnants of 190-million-year-old Pacific reefs. The caverns contain one of the largest populations of endemic cave-dwelling insects in the United States. The site also has recently gained notoriety for the discovery of a Pleistocene-age jaguar and grizzly bear fossils. Guided tours are offered from March through November and explore a ½-mile section of the underground world.

19

Lost Lake

Location: northwest face of Mount Hood, Mount Hood National Forest

Distance (round-trip): 3¼ miles

Time (round-trip): 3 hours

Vertical rise: 100 feet

Difficulty: easy

Map: USGS 7½' Bull Run Lake

Best season: late spring, summer, early fall

Lost Lake is beautiful, small and surrounded by an old-growth forest and marshland. Huge western red cedar, hemlock, and Douglas fir provide the perfect frame for Mount Hood and its reflection in the cold, clear waters of the lake.

Getting There

From Portland head east for 42 miles on US 26. Turn left on Forest Service Road 18 (Lolo Pass Road) and follow it 10½ miles to Forest Service Road 1810 (McGee Creek Road). Turn right and travel 7½ miles where you rejoin Road 18. Follow Road 18 another 7 miles to the junction of Forest Service Road 13. Turn left onto Road 13 and follow it 6 miles to the entry station. The trailhead is located in the picnic area that lies at the end of the road just past the general store.

Special Notes

This is a great family hike, with many places to access the lake. Facilities include a campground, cabins, and a general store and deli. A $5 parking fee is required.

The Trail

Known to the native tribes of the area as the "Heart of the Mountains," the trail received its current name when a surveying expedition, having trouble finding the lake, insisted that they were not lost, but, rather, that the lake was. On a clear day Mount Hood greets you across the lake with a picture-postcard view. The early morning light—just after sunrise and before the water is disturbed by swimmers—

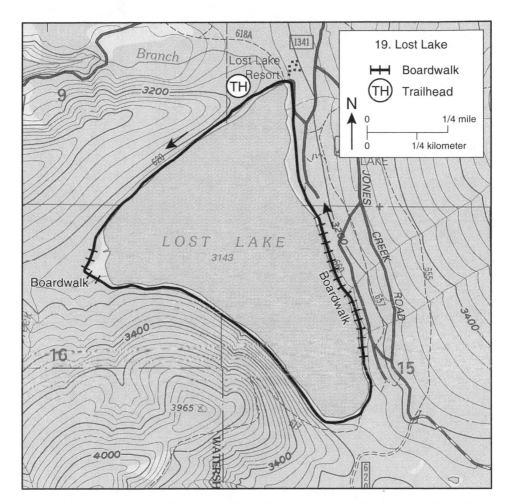

19. Lost Lake

⊢⊣ Boardwalk

(TH) Trailhead

offers a fantastic photographic opportunity. The well-used lakeside trail begins in old-growth Douglas fir, hemlock, and cedar and follows the shore around the entire lake. Along the way are numbered posts that correspond to a trail guide available at the general store.

After following the trail ½ mile, the forest begins to open up and a wide boardwalk leads across a marsh area where skunk cabbage thrives and a small creek joins the lake. After ¾ mile from the trailhead, you encounter a trail junction. The trail to the right eventually leads to the Pacific Crest Trail.

Stay to the left and soon the trail turns into a boardwalk leading through a grove of huge western red cedars. The wide boardwalk extends along the lakeshore, just below the Forest Service campground, for almost ½ mile. Along the way you find benches built into the boardwalk with views of the lake and several sets of stairs leading down to the water.

A ½ mile past the end of the boardwalk, you encounter the boat ramp, general store, and the often-crowded swimming area. After crossing the bridge, it's only a short ¼ mile back to the picnic parking area.

Mount Hood from Lolo Pass

Along the way Steller's jays, gray jays, and chipmunks may be asking for a handout. In the morning or evening, you may see an occasional osprey or bald eagle on the less-populated side of the lake. In the spring, wildflowers such as queen's cup, bunchberry, and rhododendron bring some color to the trail.

20

Cooper Spur

Location: Mount Hood National Forest

Distance (round-trip): 7¾ miles

Time (round-trip): 7 hours

Vertical gain: 2,800 feet

Difficulty: difficult

Maps: USGS 7½' Mount Hood North; USFS Mount Hood Wilderness Area

Best season: summer

Beginning at 5,800 feet and ending at 8,500 feet, this is the highest hiking trail on Mount Hood. With the height come spectacular views of eastern Washington, eastern Oregon, from Mount Rainier to the Three Sisters, and the Eliot Glacier, Oregon's largest.

Getting There
From Portland drive 55 miles east on US 26 to the intersection of OR 35. Follow OR 35 north to the Cooper Spur Ski Area turn-off and follow Cooper Spur Road 3¼ miles to Forest Service Road 3212. Follow the Forest Service road 3212 for 10 rough and winding miles to the Cloud Cap Campground and watch for the TIMBERLINE TRAIL sign.

Special Notes
Weather can change rapidly at the higher elevations, so check the forecast before starting your hike. Allow some extra time if you are not acclimated to high-elevation hiking. A Northwest Forest Pass is required to park at the trailhead and is available at the ranger station and from many private vendors ($5 daily, $30 annually).

The Trail
The trailhead is located next to the TIMBER-LINE TRAIL sign. Begin by following this trail in the direction of Gnarl Ridge as it passes through twisted white bark pine trees huddled together for protection and alpine meadows of lupine, paintbrush, and beargrass. Stay to the left at the first two trail junctions, and after 1¼ miles turn right onto

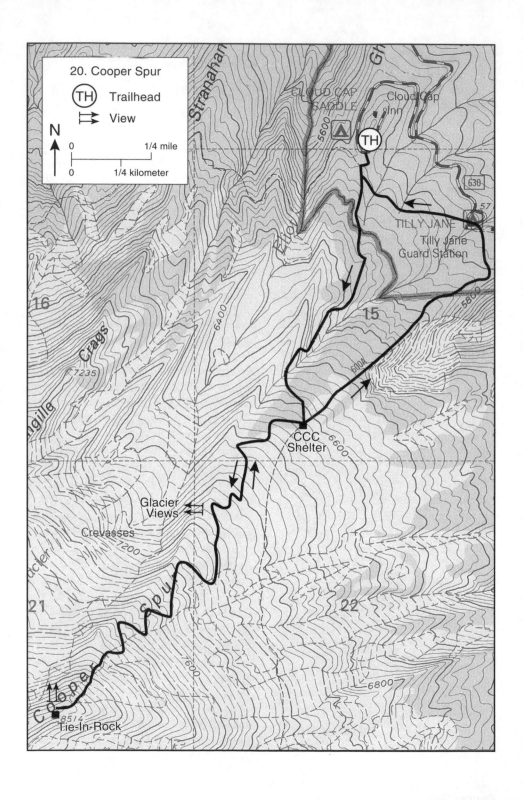

20. Cooper Spur

(TH) Trailhead
⇉ View

N

0 _____ 1/4 mile
0 _____ 1/4 kilometer

CLOUD CAP SADDLE
Cloud Cap Inn
TH
630
57
TILLY JANE
Tilly Jane Guard Station
5600
5800
16
Crags
7235
6400
15
6000
6600
CCC Shelter
Glacier Views
Crevasses
7200
6000
Cooper Spur
21
22
6800
Tie-In-Rock
8514
Cooper
Stranahan
Eliot
Langille
Glacier

Mount Hood and Cooper Spur

the Cooper Spur Trail The first trail leads to the Tilly Jane Campground, while the second trail is the continuation of the Timberline Trail. From here the trail leads up the exposed ridgeline through a series of long switchbacks up the morain. Along the way there are several viewpoints on the ridge overlooking the twisted ice of Eliot Glacier. On warm summer days you can hear the ice groan and creak as it slowly flows down the mountain.

After a little more than 2½ miles, and almost 2,000 feet up the morain, you come upon several rock windbreaks and a carved rock commemorating the 1910 Japanese climbing expedition. Tie-in-Rock lies a few hundred feet farther. The large boulder marks the place where climbers attempting the 11,239-foot summit rope up before crossing the snowfields and glaciers that lie ahead.

The view from here seems to extend forever. To the north, over Eliot Glacier, are Mount Rainier, Mount St. Helens, Mount Adams, and the high, eastern Washington desert. To the south, over Newton-Clark Glacier, lie the northern Oregon Cascades and the high eastern Oregon desert.

On your way back down, look for a short trail spur just above the junction with the Timberline Trail. A few hundred yards up, the trail leads to an old rock shelter built by the CCC (Civilian Conservation Corps) in the 1930s.

At the junction you can either turn left and retrace your route to the car or continue straight another mile along the steep and dramatic Polallie Canyon and then on to Tilly Jane Campground. In 1980 Polallie Canyon was the source of a large landslide that roared down the mountain, killing one person and destroying several miles of OR 35. From Tilly Jane it's only ½ mile back to the trail junction at Cloud Cap and your car. A few lupine and avalanche lilies grow in the shelter of the tree line of white bark pine. However, along the exposed sections of the trail morain, partridge foot and sand verbena are all that are hearty enough to grow here.

21

Elk Meadows/Gnarl Ridge

Location: Mount Hood National Forest

*Distance (round-trip): 6¾ miles,
10¼ miles*

Time (round-trip): 6 hours, 10 hours

Vertical gain: 1,200 feet, 2,200 feet

Difficulty: moderate, difficult

*Maps: USGS 7½' Dog River; USFS
Mount Hood Wilderness Area*

Best season: summer

This hike highlights the beauty of the high Cascades. Meadows filled with mountain wildflowers and sweeping vistas of Mount Hood, Mount Adams, and the north Oregon Cascades await on the southeast flanks of Mount Hood.

Getting There

From Portland drive 55 miles east on US 26 to the intersection of OR 35. Follow OR 35 north 8 miles to the well-marked Clark Creek Sno-Park Area on the left. From Hood River travel south on OR 35 for 33 miles and look for the Clark Creek Sno-Park on your right, ¼ mile north of Sherwood Campground.

Special Notes

Weather can change rapidly at higher elevations so check the forecast before starting your hike. During times of high runoff, Newton Creek may be impassable. Bring extra water and start early if you are planning to visit both Elk Meadows and Gnarl Ridge. A Northwest Forest Pass is required to park at the trailhead and is available at the ranger station and from many private vendors ($5 daily, $30 annually).

The Trail

Beargrass greets you at the trailhead, which is located on the south end of the snow park loop road. Park on the broad shoulder next to the ELK MEADOWS trailhead sign. A little more than ¼ mile after setting out you join Clark Creek. The trail follows the creek

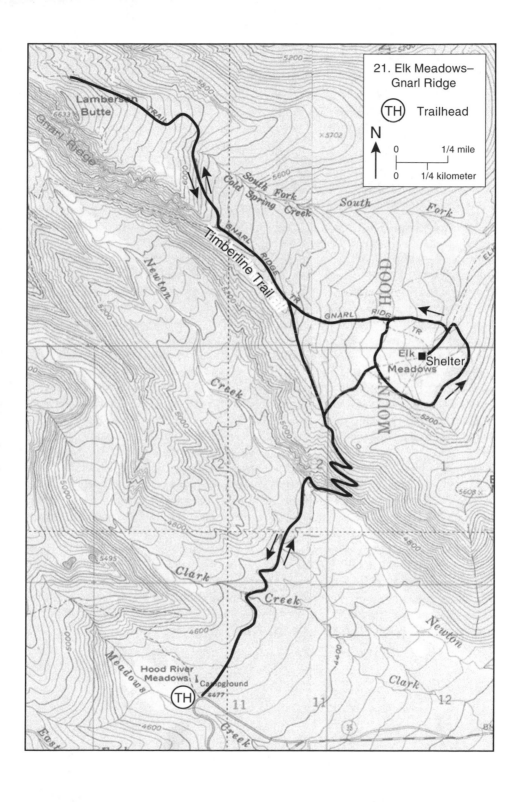

21. Elk Meadows–
Gnarl Ridge

(TH) Trailhead

N

0 _____ 1/4 mile
0 _____ 1/4 kilometer

Lamberson
Butte
6613

Gnarl Ridge

Newton
Creek

Timberline Trail

South Fork
Cold Spring Creek

GNARL RIDGE TR

×5702

5200

South

Fork

HOOD

GNARL RIDGE TR

Elk
Meadows

■ Shelter

MOUNT

5200

×5608

Clark

Creek

Newton

Clark

Hood River
Meadows
4477

Campground

(TH)

11

11

12

East

Rhododendrons along Elk Meadows Trail

for ¾ mile, where you cross over a small log footbridge and officially enter the Mount Hood National Wilderness Area. As you continue another ½ mile through Douglas fir and rhododendron sprinkled with lupine and huckleberries, you come to the Newton Creek crossing. The crossing seems to change from year to year. Be prepared to ford the creek or cross on a single log or several logs bound together to make a footbridge. Either way use caution; the water can be swift and it is always very cold.

From here the trail starts the steep mile-long climb up Gnarl Ridge through a series of switchbacks. If you are headed for Elk Meadows, hike straight through the junction at the top, and after ¼ mile you will reach the trail junction for the Elk Meadows Loop. If you are heading for Gnarl Ridge, turn left and follow the trail along the ridgeline. From here Gnarl Ridge is 2½ miles away.

The Elk Meadows Loop is 1¼ miles and circles some of the most beautiful subalpine wildflower meadows in the Oregon Cascades. Bog gentian, bog orchid, common paintbrush, monkeyflower, tiger lily, glacier lily, and columbine are just a few of the flowers that can be found amount the small tree islands of fir and pine in the meadows.

Taking a right and following the loop counterclockwise ½ mile around you come to a short trail spur to the left, which follows a small creek to the small wooden Elk Meadows shelter. If you plan to camp there are several sites along the loop trail. Camping within the meadows, however, is strictly prohibited. Continuing along the loop trail for ¼ mile brings you to another trail junction. The left fork leads to the beginning of the Elk Meadows Loop and back down to the trailhead.

If you plan to visit Gnarl Ridge, turn right and follow the trail ½ mile to the trail junction. The trail joining from the left is the Elk Meadows bypass trail. Stay to the right where, after ¼ mile, you join the Timberline Trail. Turn right and follow the pointers toward Cloud Cap.

As you follow the Timberline (or Gnarl Ridge) Trail, it soon leads you out of the tree line and into the exposed alpine region with views of Mount Adams to the north and Mount Jefferson and the Three Sisters to the south. Along the way, you'll pass the weathered and twisted trunks of white bark pines and wildflowers such as alpine aster, partridge foot, and spreading phlox. After 1½ miles you pass behind Lamberson Butte and an old rock-climbing shelter to arrive at the Gnarl Ridge overlook. From the cliff edge, the peak of Mount Hood looms over the Newton-Clark Glacier and Newton Creek in the canyon almost 1,000 feet below.

22

Tamanawas Falls

Location: *Mount Hood National Forest*

Distance (round-trip): *3¾ miles, 5¾ miles*

Time (round-trip): *3½ hours, 5½ hours*

Vertical gain: *500 feet, 850 feet*

Difficulty: *easy, moderate*

Maps: *USGS 7½' Dog River; USFS Mount Hood Wilderness Area*

Best season: *spring, summer, fall*

Tamanawas Falls makes for a great summer hike. The shaded trail winds back and forth over the aptly named Cold Spring Creek and provides a welcome break from the heat of midsummer days. At the end you are rewarded with a beautiful, broad, and curtainlike falls dropping 100 feet.

Getting There
From Portland drive 55 miles east on US 26 to the intersection of OR 35. Follow OR 35 north 18 miles to the well-marked East Fork trailhead on the left. From Hood River travel south on OR 35 for 23 miles and look for the East Fork trailhead on your right, ¼ mile north of Sherwood Campground.

Special Notes
Due to its length and easy access, this is a great family trail; however, it can become crowded during the summer months. A Northwest Forest Pass is required to park at the trailhead and is available at the ranger station and from many private vendors ($5 daily, $30 annually).

The Trail
The trailhead is located at the northwest end of the parking area where, after a few hundred yards a footbridge leads across the glacier-fed East Fork of the Hood River. Turn right onto East Fork Trail. From here the trail roughly parallels the river, although it is never in sight, through Douglas fir, western red cedar, and western hemlock. After approximately ½ mile, the trail climbs a small ridge, providing a view of the East Fork of

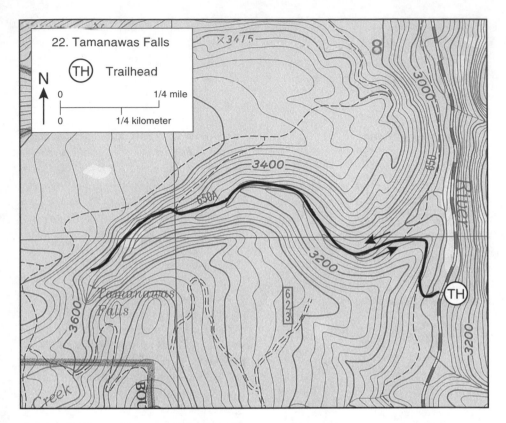

the Hood River and OR 35, before turning west to join Cold Spring Creek. A few hundred yards more brings you to the footbridge crossing the creek.

The next mile of the trail follows the creek as it tumbles over the rocks and boulders in the stream. There are also access points to the creek to cool your feet as well as several picturesque cascades as the creek passes through the fir, hemlock, and cedar forest. After 1 mile from the Cold Spring Creek footbridge, the trail forks. The right fork leads to Elk Meadows and the Polallie Overlook. Stay to the left to continue on to the falls. The old trail used to cross the creek at this point. However, a recent landslide from the overhanging cliffs, have since destroyed the trail and footbridge, the remains of which

can still be seen in the creek. The current primitive trail climbs across the landslide and over several large boulders until it picks up the old trail on the other side of the slide. From here the trail follows the base of the cliff another ¼ mile to the broad 100-foot-high falls and tumbles through a notch carved into the lip of an old basalt lava flow.

Take some time on the way back to look for trillium, fairy slipper, tiger lily, and twinflower that are common along the trail in the spring. Steller's jays, Clark's nutcrackers, American dippers, and golden-mantled ground squirrels all populate the area as well.

If you would like to extend the hike an extra 2¾ miles, try taking the loop to the Polallie Overlook and back along the East Fork of the Hood River. Returning from the

Cascade Range

Tamanawas Falls and trail

falls, turn left at the Elk Meadows trail junction and stay to the right. After another uneventful 1 ½ miles, you come to a short trail spur to the left leading to the Polallie Overlook. From here you can look down onto Polallie Creek. In 1980 heavy rains triggered a massive landslide and flash flood that originated several miles upstream. The slide tore through the old-growth forest below killing one person and destroying several miles of OR 35.

Rejoining the main trail, it's another 1 ¼ miles past the Polallie parking area and along the boulder-strewn and milky waters of the Hood River East Fork before you come to the junction of the East Fork Trail. From here it's only ½ mile back to the trailhead parking area.

23

Ramona Falls

Location: Mount Hood National Forest

Distance (round-trip): 7 miles

Time (round-trip): 5 hours

Vertical gain: 1,000 feet

Difficulty: moderate

Maps: USGS 7½' Bull Run Lake; USFS Mount Hood Wilderness Area

Best season: spring, summer, fall

Nestled in a cool forest of Douglas fir, 120-foot Ramona Falls is a fan-shaped cascade that tumbles over an ancient columnar basalt lava flow.

Getting There

From Portland drive 40 miles east on US 26 to Zigzag. Turn left onto Lolo Pass Road and follow it 5 miles to Forest Service Road 1825. Turn onto 1825 and follow it for 2¾ miles, across the Sandy River bridge, to spur road 1825-100. Turn left onto spur road 1825-100 and follow it to the trailhead.

Special Notes

The temporary footbridge over the Sandy River is in place from April to October. Store your valuables in a secure place as this parking area has had problems with break-ins. A Northwest Forest Pass is required to park at the trailhead and is available at the ranger station and from many private vendors ($5 daily, $30 annually).

The Trail

The trailhead is located on the east end of the large, gravel parking area. The trail begins in a relatively young Douglas fir and western hemlock forest, with a carpet of moss covering the round rocks and boulders left behind by the numerous Sandy River floods and mudflows and Mount Hood eruptions. Soon you join the alder-lined Sandy River and in a little more than ¼ mile you ford a small seasonal stream. The Sandy is a glacial stream that begins at the Reid and Sandy Glaciers located only a few

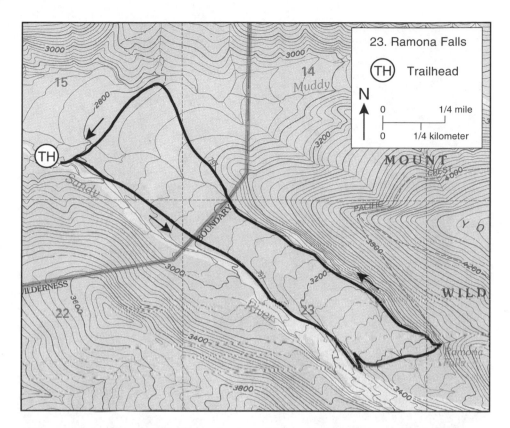

miles upstream. The river's milky color is caused by glacial silt. The glaciers, with their tremendous weight, slowly ground the rock into a fine powder, which was then washed downstream by the melting waters—and still does today.

After 1¼ miles from the trailhead you cross the Sandy over a seasonal bridge placed by the National Forest Service each spring and removed each fall. Almost immediately after you cross the seasonal bridge you come to the first trail junction. From the bridge, Mount Hood towers over the river, making a great photo opportunity at sunrise or sunset. The left fork of the trail is a horse path that can be used for the return trip. Turn right and after a few hundred yards you will cross the crystal clear waters of Ramona Creek. Continuing on for another ½ mile brings you to another junction; the trail to the left leads across the Muddy Fork of the Sandy River and on up to Lolo Pass where it eventually joins the Timberline Trail. Turn right, and after a ½ mile through fir and, in the spring, beautiful pink and red rhododendron, you arrive back at the mossy rocks of Ramona Creek. From here the falls is only a mile away, and you officially enter the Mount Hood Wilderness Area and the old-growth forest composed of huge Douglas fir and western red cedar. To the left, just across the creek, are the old basalt cliffs that will form the base of the falls. A few hundred yards before the falls, the trail crosses the creek on a small footbridge and gently climbs a small slope to a junction for the

Ramona Falls and trail bridge

Yocum Ridge Trail. Stay to the right where the trail then dips down to once again cross the creek on a scenic wooden footbridge just in front of the falls. On a hot summer day, the cool mist is a refreshing treat.

Ramona Falls is 120 feet high and cascades over a columnar basalt lava flow that in part forms the base of Mount Hood's volcanic cone. The flow dates back to between 500,000 and 700,000 years ago, during the early years of Mount Hood's growth.

On the return trip you can either go back the way you came, which I recommend, or continue the loop by turning right and crossing the creek.

About ½ mile after you turn back, the trail rejoins the Sandy River, which it then parallels for 2 miles back to the seasonal bridge.

The last major eruption of Mount Hood occurred in 1790 during a span of activity known as the "Old Maid Period." The eruptions produced several mud flows. The evidence of one of these flows can still be seen in the stunted forest and moss-covered boulders you encounter along the Sandy River portion of the trail.

24

Silver Falls

Location: Silver Falls State Park

Distance (round-trip): ½ miles

Time (round-trip): 5 hours

Vertical rise: 600 feet

Difficulty: easy

Maps: USGS 7½' Drake Crossing; Silver Falls State Park brochure

Best season: spring, fall, winter

The Silver Creek Canyon Trail leads through moss-covered second-growth Douglas fir, hemlock, and cedar as it passes by, and sometimes behind, 10 spectacular waterfalls ranging in height from 27 to 178 feet.

Getting There

From Salem drive 10 miles east on OR 22 to CR 214. Travel north 15 miles on OR 214, following the SILVER FALLS STATE PARK signs, to the park. Turn left into the South Falls/swimming area parking lot.

Special Notes

The falls are at their peak during the spring, fall, and winter months. Summer weekends can be very crowded. An Oregon Parks day-use fee is required and is available at the entrance booth, as well as from many private vendors ($3 daily, $25 annually).

The Trail

Silver Falls is Oregon's largest state park, encompassing 8,700 acres. The first European to discover the area was fur trapper Donald McKenzie in about 1810. In the 1930s the state began acquiring land from the region's early settlers, who had built a small mining and lumber camp named Silver Falls City. The area was officially dedicated as a state park in 1933. In 1935 a Civilian Conservation Corps (CCC) camp was established near North Falls and work began on many of the park's facilities, including a boys' camp and lodge, which was listed on the National Register of Historic Places in 1983.

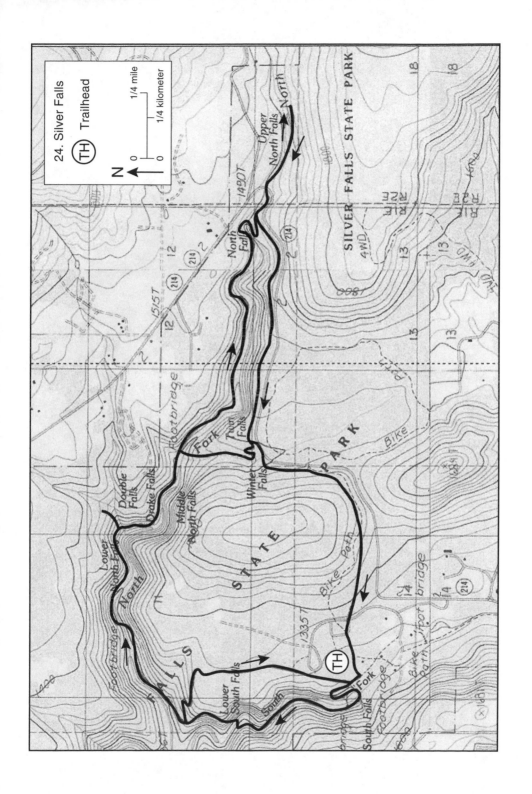

24. Silver Falls

(TH) Trailhead

N

0   1/4 mile
0   1/4 kilometer

SILVER FALLS STATE PARK

Upper North Falls

North

North Falls

214

214

1490T

1800

1900

214

2

North Fork

Footbridge

Double Falls

Drake Falls

Lower North Falls

Middle North Falls

Twin Falls

Winter Falls

STATE

PARK

Bike Path

1335T

Bike Path

14

214

1400

Footbridge

South Fork

Lower South Falls

South

Footbridge

Bike Foot bridge

Footbridge

South Falls

R1E R2E

SILVER FALLS STATE PARK

4WD

13

13

13

18

18

4WD R70

North Falls from the Canyon Trail

The trail begins at the South Falls rim and switchbacks down to its base. From here the trail then leads behind the falls and under the basalt lava flow that creates the 177-foot falls. The cave was created when the softer sediment lying beneath the basalt eroded away.

From here the trail continues past the footbridge and along the South Fork of Silver Creek where, after another ¾ mile, it brings you to a viewpoint of the 93-foot curtain of Lower South Falls. The trail crosses the creek behind the falls where, after ¼ mile, you encounter a trail junction. If you are short on time, take the right fork, which, after 1 mile, leads up the rim and back to the parking lot. Following the Canyon Trail straight through maple, alder, and fir, you soon come to the North Fork of Silver Creek. The trail crosses the creek on a small footbridge and leads to the 30-foot punchbowl of Lower North Falls. At the footbridge, just above the falls, take the short trail to the left. The short spur follows Hullt creek a few hundred yards to Double Falls. This delicate, 178-foot-high ribbon is the tallest of the falls in the park.

Crossing the footbridge over Hullt Creek and following the main trail another ¼ mile brings you to Drake Falls, the park's smallest. The 27-foot cascade is named after June Drake, an early naturalist and photographer of the area. The next waterfall along the trail is the 106-foot curtain of Middle North Falls. A short trail to the right will lead you behind the falls.

One-quarter mile past Middle North Falls the trail again forks. If you wish to return at this point, take the Winter Falls cut-off trail to the right. Follow it across the footbridge and up a steep ½ mile to the junction of the Canyon Trail at the top of Winter Falls. Turn right, rejoining the Canyon Trail, and follow the trail back to the South Falls parking area

1½ miles away. Follow the right fork across the footbridge and climb the rim to the Winter Falls wayside. From here, follow the Canyon Trail back to the South Falls parking area.

Twin Falls is the next waterfall you encounter if you continue along the creek. It's a 31-foot-tall, punchbowl-style cascade that is split into two streams by the protruding rocks at the top of the falls.

From here it is 1 mile through ferns and moss-covered maple, alder, fir, and vine maple, to the most spectacular waterfall in the park, North Falls. Here the water has cut a single narrow channel into the basalt leading to a dramatic 136-foot plunge. The trail continues through a huge cavern behind the falls. In the basalt roof of the cave above are deep circular holes. These holes are actually casts of the ancient trees living here when the lava flowed around them 15 million years ago. The wood then burned or rotted away over time leaving only the cast.

From here the trail steeply climbs the cliff next to the falls and follows the creek to another trail junction near the North Falls parking area. Take the ½-mile trail spur to the left and follow it under the bridge to Upper North Falls, a 65-foot-high curtain that tumbles into a large pool often frequented by swimmers.

From the North Falls junction, follow the trail along the rim 1 mile to the Winter Falls wayside. Winter Falls is a 134-foot seasonal falls. As its name implies, it is best observed in the winter months or during times of heavy runoff. From here the trail roughly parallels the park road through secondgrowth fir, hemlock, and cedar with an undergrowth of Oregon grape, salal, sword, and bracken fern for 1½ miles back to the South Falls parking area.

Approximately 25 million years ago this area was part of the Pacific coastline. The soft sandstone, evident behind many of the falls, is actually ancient beach sand that is part of the Scotts Mills Formation. Continental forces gradually lifted the land upwards, and around 15 million years ago, huge fissures in eastern Washington and Oregon erupted, resulting in the Columbia River basalt lava flows that covered the area.

25

Opal Creek

Location: Opal Creek Wilderness Area

Distance (round-trip): 7 miles

Time (round-trip): 5 hours

Vertical rise: 400 feet

Difficulty: easy

Map: USGS 7½' Elkhorn, Battle Ax

Best season: spring, summer, fall

The cold, clear, pristine waters of Opal Creek and the Little North Santiam River pass by huge old-growth Douglas fir trees and an old, well-preserved gold mine.

Getting There

From Salem travel east on US 22 (North Santiam Highway) 23 miles to the small town of Mehama. Turn left onto Little North Fork Road and follow it 15 miles where it turns to gravel and another 1¼ miles to the intersection of Forest Service Road 2209 and Forest Service Road 2207. Take the left fork (Road 2209) and follow it 6 miles to the locked gate and the start of the trailhead.

Special Notes

Jawbone Flats maintains a resident population. Respect residents' privacy by staying on the road. A Northwest Forest Pass is required to park at the trailhead and is available at the ranger station and from many private vendors ($5 daily, $30 annually).

The Trail

Archeological evidence shows that the clear, cold waters of the Opal Creek area have been known to Native Americans for more than 2,000 years. Nearby Whetstone Mountain was a vision-quest destination and the Whetstone Mountain Trail a frequent trade route for the local tribes.

The trail begins at the locked gate and follows the old dirt service road above the Little North Santiam River. After following the road for a little less than ½ mile, you cross the Gold Creek Bridge built in 1939.

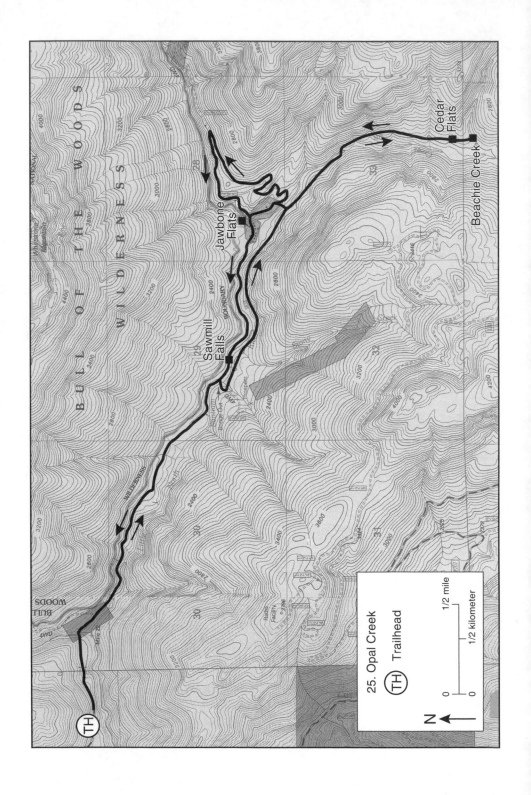

25. Opal Creek

(TH) Trailhead

N

| 0 | | 1/2 mile |
| 0 | | 1/2 kilometer |

Three pools on the Little North Santiam River, Opal Creek

The road then clings to the rock cliffs above the river through a section known as Half Bridge. From here you begin to enter the old-growth forest. Many of these trees reach a height of 250 feet and an age of between 500 and 1,000 years. These trees were at the heart of one of the most heated environmental battles in the nation. Throughout the late 1980s and mid-1990s, environmentalists and the timber industry squared off in the forest and in the courtroom until the U.S. Congress created the 20,300-acre Opal Creek Wilderness Area in 1996.

At the 2-mile mark you come to the remnants of the old Merten Mill. Using equipment salvaged from the battleship USS *Oregon,* the mill provided lumber for the area's mines. A short trail to the right leads to the broad 30-foot Cascadia de los Niños (Waterfall of the Children) where the Little North Santiam River cascades into a large opalescent pool.

After continuing along the road for another ¼ mile, you come to a trail that branches off to the right. Take the right fork and cross over the river on a log bridge into the Opal Creek Scenic Recreation Area and to where the Opal Creek Trail begins. After crossing the river follow the trail to the left as it follows the river for 1½ miles, crossing over Stormy Creek, and on to scenic Slide Falls on the Little North Santiam River. After passing Slide Falls, the trail briefly leaves the river and crosses over a fir-, hemlock-, and cedar-forested bench. After ¾ mile the trail rejoins the river and overlooks the gemlike waters of Opal Pool nestled in a scenic gorge. Turn left at the trail junction and cross the bridge just above Opal Pool. Follow the trail to the old mining road and turn left into Jawbone Flats.

Gold was found in the area in 1859, bringing miners from all around to try their luck. In 1931 the Jawbone Flats Mining Camp was established by James Hewitt. The camp produced moderate quantities of gold, silver, zinc, and lead until 1992, when the Shiny Rock Mining Company donated it to The Friends of Opal Creek. Two dozen well-maintained buildings remain and now acts as an old-growth-forest study center.

From Jawbone Flats follow the old service road 3½ miles back to the trailhead. On your way, look for the dominate understory of huckleberry, vine maple, and rhododendron. Wildlife common to the area include black bear, coyote, elk, deer, eagles, and spotted owls.

If you would like to extend your hike an extra 3¼ miles, continue along the trail past Opal Pool and follow it along Opal Creek. After ½ mile the trail crosses the creek and passes a small cascade. Continuing on for another mile, you pass several more scenic cascades before arriving at Cedar Flats, which derives its name from the cluster of old cedar trees near the edge of the flats. A few hundred yards farther brings you to Beachie Creek and the trail's end.

26

Sahalie Falls

Location: Near McKenzie Bridge, Willamette National Forest

Distance (round-trip): 1½ miles

Time (round-trip): 1 hour

Vertical rise: 200 feet

Difficulty: easy

Maps: USGS 7½' Linton Lake; Three Sisters Wilderness (Geo-Graphics)

Best season: late spring, summer, early fall

This short trail takes you past two highly different waterfalls and through an example of Oregon's dense rain forest.

Getting There
From Eugene travel east on OR 126 to McKenzie Bridge. Continue east through McKenzie Bridge 19 miles on US 126 to the Sahalie Falls Rest Area on the left.

Special Notes
The waterfalls are at their highest flow in the spring. Due to its length and easy access, the section of the trail around Sahalie Falls can become crowded during the summer months. No permits or fees are required.

The Trail
Cascading over moss-covered lava, this section of the McKenzie River creates an atmosphere that briefly takes you back to a time before today's complicated life. You view the river much as it appeared to the early Native Americans.

A small information kiosk is located at the parking area and offers information describing the region's geology and Native American history.

The trail begins on the east side of the large paved parking area. From here stay to the right and follow the paved trail a short ¼ mile to a railed viewpoint at the rim of the falls. At this point you can witness the cold, clear blue waters of the McKenzie River rush by your feet to plunge 100 feet to the moss-covered rocks below. Retrace your steps and turn right at the junction where,

Sahalie Falls, from lower viewpoint

after a few hundred feet, you come to the misty lower viewpoint. From here you can better see the basalt lava flow that, a little more than 6,000 years ago, squeezed the river into this narrow channel.

As you continue along the trail, the pavement soon ends, and you pass through large old-growth Douglas fir and western red cedar with an undergrowth of Oregon grape and sword and bracken fern beside the churning waters of the McKenzie. American dippers are often feeding in the water, while the woodpecker-like northern flickers can often be seen among the trees.

Follow the trail along the river for ½ mile from Sahalie Falls where you come to the rim of the 80-foot-high Koosah Falls. A short spur to the left leads down to the observation point for a view of the falls. Unlike Sahalie Falls, Koosah Falls is a very broad curtain that plunges into a well-defined pool. If you look carefully, you can see many small springs flowing from the porous lava at the base of the falls.

From here you can either turn around and retrace you steps back to the Sahalie Falls parking area or continue following the river another ½ mile to the trail's end at the Carman Reservoir Road.

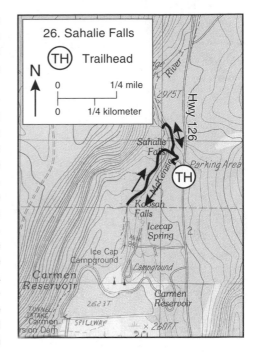

26. Sahalie Falls

TH Trailhead

N

0 ——— 1/4 mile

0 ——— 1/4 kilometer

27

Proxy Falls

Location: Three Sisters Wilderness Area

Distance (round-trip): 1½ miles

Time (round-trip): 1 hour

Vertical rise: 200 feet

Difficulty: easy

Maps: USGS 7½' Linton Lake; Three Sisters Wilderness (Geo-Graphics)

Best season: late spring, summer, early fall

Proxy Falls Trail is located along one of Oregon's many scenic byways, just inside the northwest border of the Three Sisters Wilderness Area. Both Upper and Lower Proxy Falls cascade over basalt cliffs carved by the last Ice Age approximately 8,000 years ago.

Getting There

From Eugene travel east on OR 126 to the junction of OR 242 (McKenzie Pass Scenic Bi-way). After approximately 9 miles a hiker sign and roadside parking area designate the trailhead. From Salem travel east on US 20 and then south on OR 126 to the OR 242 junction.

Special Notes

The waterfalls are at their highest flow in the spring. Owing to its length and easy access, this trail can become crowded during the summer months. A Northwest Forest Pass is required to park at the trailhead and is available at the ranger station and from many private vendors ($5 daily, $30 annually).

The Trail

This short but highly enjoyable trail is a loop with two short spurs to each of the falls. From the parking lot, walk to the right where the trail starts by crossing over a 4,500-year-old lava flow from cinder cones near the North Sister. The flow is composed of jumbled rocks, which, in the fall, are covered in moss and vine maple, providing a great splash of color. Where they can find a foothold, the occasional old-growth Douglas fir or hemlock

Lower Proxy Falls

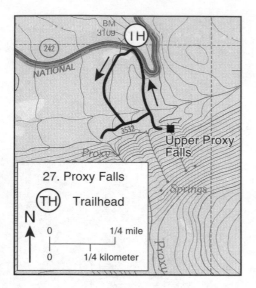

27. Proxy Falls

(TH) Trailhead

N

0 ——————— 1/4 mile

0 ——————— 1/4 kilometer

towers above all. The trail forks after crossing the lava. A few hundred yards down the right fork at the Lower Proxy Falls viewpoint, the trail ends. Douglas fir, hemlock, and cedar trees frame the view of the falls as it cascades 130 feet down the stepped face of the glacier-carved basalt cliff.

Continuing along the main trail, you'll pass through old-growth western hemlock, Douglas fir, and yew trees. A spring hike will yield blooming rhododendron, vanilla leaf, Oregon grape, and the occasional Oregon iris. At the second fork, bear right for a few hundred yards to the smaller Upper Proxy Falls. The trail ends at the collection pool formed at the base of the falls, which has no visible outlet. The water flows through the porous lava and emerges at the springs, creating Lost Creek and White Branch Creek located several miles down the canyon. The narrow upper falls cascades 120 feet down the same basalt cliff as the lower falls but with half the volume.

From the upper falls' collection pool, it's only a ½-mile hike back to the trailhead. From the junction of the main trail and the upper falls' spur, turn right and follow the trail over the lava and back to the parking area.

Ravens, woodpeckers, Steller's jays, Clarks nutcrackers, and various songbirds all frequent the area as do mule and white-tailed deer, chipmunks, Douglas' squirrels, and raccoons. Also frequenting the area but rarely seen are black bear, bobcat, and mountain lion.

28

Tam McArthur Rim

Location: Three Sisters Wilderness Area

Distance (round-trip): 7¼ miles

Time (round-trip): 6 hours

Vertical rise: 1,600 feet

Difficulty: moderate

Map: USGS 7½' Tumalo Falls, Broken Top

Best season: summer, early fall

The Tam McArthur Rim trail offers one of the best views into the high central Oregon Cascades. From the many viewpoints along the rim you can take a moment to look straight into the heart of the Broken Top and the Three Sisters.

Getting There
From Sisters travel south on Elm Street, which turns into Three Creek Road (Forest Service Road 16). After 17 miles you come to the entrance of Driftwood Campground. Look for the trailhead sign just to the left of the entrance.

Special Notes
Weather can change rapidly at higher ele-vations, so check the forecast before start-ing your hike. Allow some extra time if you are not acclimated to high-elevation hiking. A Northwest Forest Pass is required to park at the trailhead and is available at the ranger station and from many private vendors ($5 daily, $30 annually).

The Trail
The rim is named for Lewis "Tam" McArthur who was appointed to the Oregon Geo-graphic Board by Governor Oswald West in 1914 and served as its secretary from 1916 to 1949.

From the trailhead, located on the left side of the road, the trail immediately begins a steep 1-mile climb into the Three Sisters Wilderness Area above Three Creek Lake to the plateau rim. Along the way you will begin in lodgepole pine, pass through a

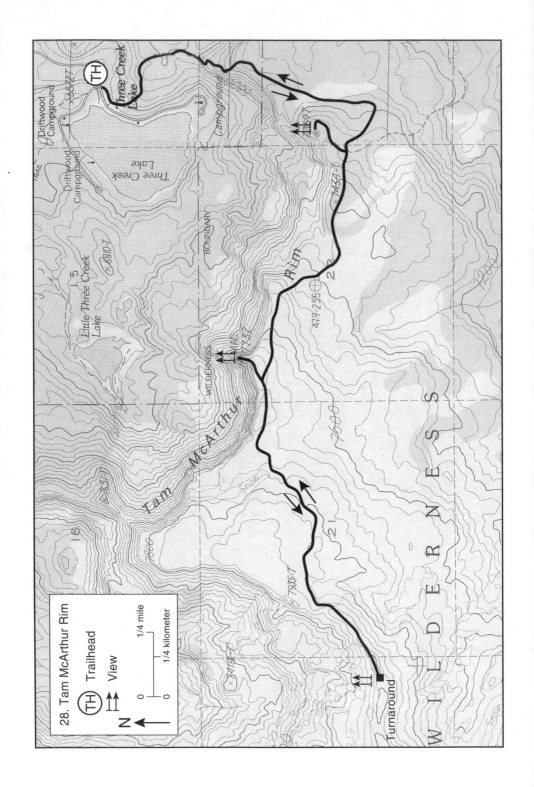

28. Tam McArthur Rim

(TH) Trailhead

↑↑ View

N ←

0 ——— 1/4 mile
0 ——— 1/4 kilometer

Three Creek Lake

Driftwood Campground

Driftwood Campground

Three Creek Lake

Little Three Creek Lake

Tam McArthur Rim

BOUNDARY

WILDERNESS

W I L D E R N E S S

Snow

Snow

Snow

Turnaround

Tam McArthur Rim over Three Creek Lake

region of mountain hemlock, and enter the realm of white bark pine, which populates the ash and pumice soils of the alpine plateau.

An early morning or late afternoon hike may offer a glimpse of a porcupine, which are abundant throughout the region. Additional wildlife includes elk, deer, and, in the higher elevations along the trail, martins and marmots. In the skies look for bald eagles and hawks.

Once on the plateau, the trail begins to level off and views of Mount Washington, Three Fingered Jack, and Mount Jefferson begin to unfold.

At the 2½-mile point, a small spur leads a few hundred yards to the right and a viewpoint on a stagelike extension of the plateau. At an elevation of 7,700 feet, there is a a magnificent and direct view into the heart of the central Oregon Cascades as they all line up—from Broken Top and the Three Sisters to Mount Washington, Mount Jefferson, Mount

Hood, and, on a clear day, Mount Adams in Washington State. To the east the view extends from Three Creek Lake and little Three Creek Lake 1,000 feet below, across the high desert to the Ochoco Mountains in the distance.

Continuing along the main trail for another 1¼ miles through clusters of white bark pine, you come to a small red cinder cone that marks the end of the plateau. The plateau is covered in snow much of the year. Even in the summer months you are likely to encounter snowfields along this part of the trail. Use caution when traversing them.

The trail becomes less defined as it makes its way to the base of Broken Hand a mile away. Here you can look across to Broken Top and down onto the Crook Glacier in the huge eroded crater bowl.

At this point the hiking ends and the rock climbing begins. Unless you are experienced in climbing and have the proper equipment, don't attempt to traverse the steep and slippery cliffs of Broken Hand.

During July and August a surprising array of wildflowers populate porous volcanic soil. Look for common paintbrush, lupine, alpine aster, sulfur plant, and the pungent, little, fuzzy, white dirty socks. These flowers grow in clusters to conserve water.

29

South Sister

Location: Three Sisters Wilderness Area

Distance (round-trip): 12 miles

Time (one-way): 10 hours

Vertical rise: 4,900 feet

Difficulty: very difficult

Map: USGS 7½' South Sister, Broken Top

Best season: summer

Standing at 10,358 feet, the South Sister, nicknamed "Charity," is the third highest peak in Oregon. Although much taller than other mountains, and requiring climbing skills and equipment, the summit of South Sister can be reached by the determined hiker and lung power alone.

Getting There

From Bend drive 27 miles west on OR 46 (Cascade Lakes Highway), following the signs to the Mount Bachelor Ski Area. Travel past the Ski Area 6½ miles to Devils Lake Campground on the left. The trailhead is located at the far end of the campground loop.

Special Notes

Weather can change rapidly at higher elevations, so check the forecast prior to starting your hike. Take extra water and allow for extra time if you are not acclimated to high-elevation hiking. A Northwest Forest Pass is required to park at the trailhead and is available from many private vendors ($5 daily, $30 annually).

The Trail

The South Sister is the tallest and youngest of the Three Sisters. It is classified as a *stratovolcano,* a conical volcano made from a composite cone of lava and ash, and began erupting approximately 200,000 years ago. The craters at the summit were created at the end of the last Ice Age, approximately 8,000 years ago. Rock Mesa and Devils Hill

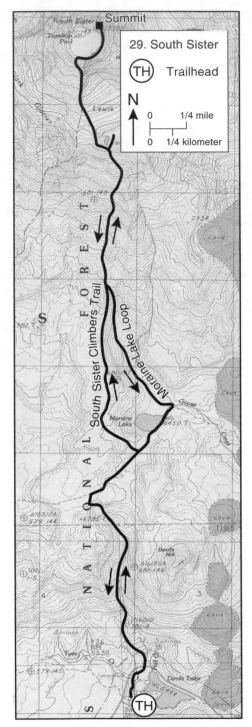

29. South Sister

(TH) Trailhead

N

0   1/4 mile

0   1/4 kilometer

to the east represent some of the most recent activity in the area, occurring 2,000 years ago. While the volcano is considered dormant, it is by no means extinct. Recent measurements indicate that a 100-square-kilometer area on the west flank of the mountain is beginning to rise, indicating that the mountain is possibly beginning to awaken from its 2,000-year slumber.

From the campground follow South Sister Climbers Trail, crossing Tyee Creek on a small footbridge and then across the Cascade Lakes Highway. The trail begins a steep climb through moss-covered hemlock, fir, and pine. After 1½ miles the forest opens onto a large pumice plain and views of South Sister and Broken Top. Another ¼ mile along the dusty and exposed plain brings you to a trail intersection. The trail to the right leads ¾ mile to Moraine Lake, while the left trail leads to the Wickiup Plain 1¼ miles away. To continue up the mountain, follow South Sister Climbers Trail straight.

The trail continues along on the pumice plain for another 1¾ miles to the upper junction of the Moraine Lake trail at an elevation of 7,200 feet. Along the way the twisted and weathered trunks of white bark pines and a few subalpine firs dot the landscape along with dogbane, lupine, and paintbrush. On this route are several false trails leading across the plain that should be ignored. Most of the trails are poorly defined, and the main trail is easy to follow as it cuts through the pumice. Below the ridgeline lie the green waters of Moraine Lake and to the southeast is Rock Mesa.

If you are tired and would like to leave a summit attempt for another day, turn right onto the Moraine Lake Loop and follow the steep and slippery trail 1¼ miles down to the lake and the intersection with the Green Lakes Trail. After ½ mile you encounter a trail

South Sister

leading to the left. Stay to the right and by-pass the left fork, which you will see rejoin-ing the main trail in about ½ mile. From the shores of the lake, you can enjoy lunch and wonderful views of South Sister and Broken Top. The Lewis Glacier, visible near the summit, carved the valley in which the lake lay during the last Ice Age. To return back to the Devils Lake trailhead, follow the Green Lakes Trail west ¾ mile to the previous four-way intersection and turn left. From here the trailhead is only 1½ miles away.

If you are continuing on to the summit, over the next 1¼ miles the grade steepens dramatically. Along the way you will cross sections of rhyodacite rock polished by gla-ciers during the last Ice Age. The trail levels off slightly after 1 mile as it reaches the terminal moraine of the Lewis Glacier and a small green cirque lake.

From here the trail once again steepens as you climb along the ridge between the Lewis and Clark Glacier. After ¾ mile of steep climbing through loose pumice and scree, you reach the rim of the summit crater. The trail follows the eastern edge of the rim to the short final assent of the summit.

To the north lie Green Lakes, Broken Top, Middle, and North Sister. On a clear day Mount Jefferson, Mount Hood, and Mount Adams are also visible. To the south are Mount Bachelor, Diamond Peak and, at the base of the summit crater, Teardrop Pool, Oregon's highest lake.

South Sister

30

Salt Creek Falls

Location: Willamette National Forest

Distance (round-trip): 3½ miles

Time (round-trip): 2½ hours

Vertical rise: 400 feet

Difficulty: easy

Map: USGS 7½' Diamond Peak

Best season: spring, summer, fall

Two very different waterfalls are highlighted in this pleasant family hike. Salt Creek Falls is an awe-inspiring show of nature's brute force, while Diamond Creek Falls displays a more delicate side.

Getting There
From Eugene travel east on OR 58. Approximately 1 mile past the tunnel, near milepost 66, look for the U.S. FOREST SERVICE sign for Salt Creek Falls on your right.

Special Notes
This is a very popular trail and can become quite busy during the summer months. A Northwest Forest Pass is required to park at the trailhead and is available at the ranger station and from many private vendors ($5 daily, $30 annually).

The Trail
At the turnaround is a restroom and an information booth that tells the story of the falls' creation and history. Begin the hike by first stretching your legs with a short walk downstream to the railed overlook, which offers an impressive view of the falls from the basalt rim. At 286 feet, Salt Creek Falls is the second-highest in the state behind the 542-foot Multnomah Falls. Continue past the rim viewpoint and follow the well-maintained path as it switchbacks through Douglas fir and hemlock ½ mile down to a second railed viewpoint. The viewpoint is located above the moss-covered rocks of a splash pool at the base of the cliff. From here you can feel the cool spray of the falls,

Salt Creek Falls

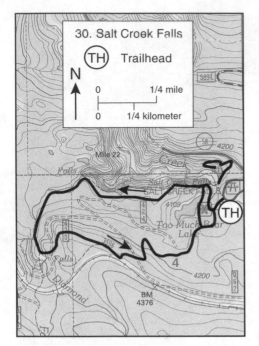

30. Salt Creek Falls

(TH) Trailhead

N

0   1/4 mile

0   1/4 kilometer

as well as having a great view of the falls as it tumbles over the cliff.

To continue on to Diamond Falls, retrace your steps back up to the rim viewpoint and follow the paved path upstream along the creek. The trailhead begins upstream where you cross Salt Creek on a small footbridge. Follow the trail a few hundred feet to the junction and turn right. After ¼ mile you come to a viewpoint overlooking the Salt Creek Canyon, and a few more steps bring

you to a short trail that forks to the left, which leads to the shallow mosquito haven of Too Much Bear Lake. From here the trail continues along the canyon rim for another mile where you will encounter several viewpoints with great photographic opportunities of both the canyon and falls. Rhododendrons are abundant along the trail during the early spring.

About 1¾ miles from the trailhead, you encounter a steep trail to the right that leads ¼ mile down to a footbridge crossing Diamond Creek. The trail then continues through a moss- and fern-covered narrow canyon and ends at the 100-foot Diamond Creek Falls. In contrast to the dramatic plunge of Salt Creek Falls, Diamond Creek Falls fans out over a stepped basalt face. Bluebells, salmonberry, monkeyflower, and bleeding heart can be found along the trail.

Returning to the main trail, turn right and follow the steep switchbacks to the next trail junction. The right trail leads into the Diamond Peak Wilderness Area along Fall Creek where you encounter Fall Creek Falls after ¼ mile, and Vivian Lake another mile past the falls. From the junction you can either return by the same route you came or turn left and follow the path 1¼ miles, twice crossing a gravel service road, to complete the loop, keeping an eye out for jays and chipmunks.

31

Metolius River

Location: Opal Creek Wilderness Area

Distance (round-trip): 5½ miles

Time (round-trip): 4½ hours

Vertical rise: 100 feet

Difficulty: easy

Map: USGS 7½' Black Butte, Candle Creek, Prairie Farm Springs

Best season: spring, summer, fall

A full-fledged river, the Metolius springs from the base of the Black Butte cinder cone. The cold, clear waters of the Metolius also produce a healthy run of rainbow trout.

Getting There
From Sisters drive west on US 20, 9 miles, to Forest Service Road 14 (Camp Sherman). Follow Road 14 approximately 10½ miles to the Wizard Falls Fish Hatchery on the left.

Special Notes
On weekends during the summer months, the trail and fish hatchery can become fairly crowded. No fees or passes are required.

The Trail
The Wizard Falls Fish Hatchery is an excellent place to warm up before your hike or cool down and have lunch at the end of your hike. The hatchery was opened in 1948. Under the large ponderosa pine and cedar trees are various holding tanks that contain as many as 3 million rainbow, brook, and brown trout, as well as kokanee and Atlantic salmon. A large holding pond at the back of the hatchery contains some extremely large trout. Food machines are placed around the pond for those interested in feeding the fish and getting a closer look.

The trail begins just before the bridge along the west bank of the Metolius River and heads up-river past Wizard Falls. Wizard Falls is, in truth, only a mild rapid. Here the river tumbles over a small ledge and into a deep channel creating the illusion

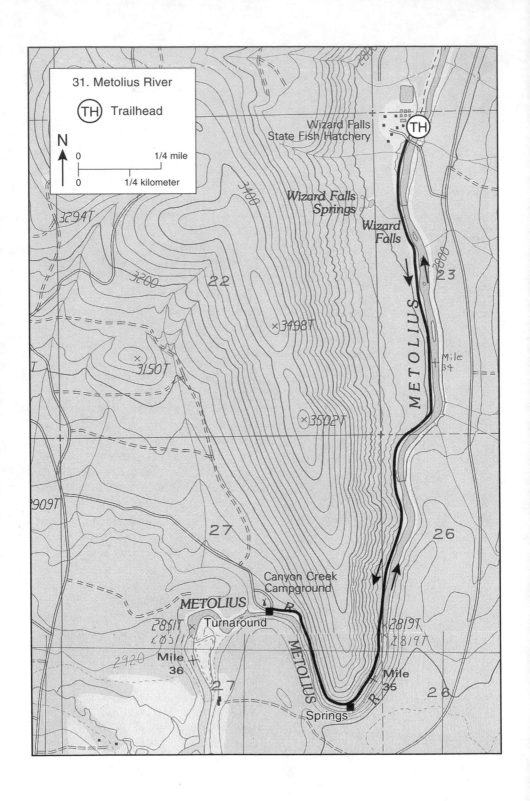

31. Metolius River

(TH) Trailhead

N

0 ——————— 1/4 mile
0 ——————— 1/4 kilometer

Wizard Falls
State Fish Hatchery

Wizard Falls
Springs

Wizard
Falls

3400

3294T

3200

22

×3498T

×3150T

×3502T

METOLIUS

Mile
34

2800

23

2909T

27

26

Canyon Creek
Campground

METOLIUS
Turnaround

R.

285T
285T

28/9T
28/9T

2920

Mile
36

METOLIUS

R.

Mile
35

26

27

Springs

Wizard Falls

of a bright aqua strip down the center of the river. The best view of the falls is from the sidewalk on the bridge.

The trail is well worn from the many fishermen who work the waters in search of that trophy trout. As you continue along, the river winds its way through a series of small islands. Ducks, American dippers, red-winged blackbirds, and Steller's jays can all be seen as they dart from the islands to shore. Also in the area are the reclusive white-headed woodpeckers, which fly from tree to tree looking for insects in the bark of ponderosa pines. Continuing still farther, the trail enters the canyon with small springs emerging through the porous lava at its base, often muddying the trail. Large, old-growth ponderosa pine covers the canyon walls. In the spring and early summer months, wildflowers abound and include larkspur, monkeyflower, columbine, and lupine.

At the 2½-mile mark near the river's bend, a huge spring gushes from the ground on the far bank and enters the river. From here it's only ¼ mile to the turnaround point at the Lower Canyon Creek Campground.

No trip to the Metolius is complete without a visit to the headwaters located 4 miles from the intersection of US 20 on Forest Service Road 14. A short, ¼-mile trail leads from the parking area through the ponderosa pine forest to a low bluff at the base of Black Butte. From here, and quite literally, springs the Metolius River.

32

Susan Creek Falls

Location: Umpqua National Forest

Distance (round-trip): 2¼ miles

Time (round-trip): 1½ hours

Vertical rise: 300 feet

Difficulty: easy

Map: USGS 7½' Old Fairview, Mace Mount

Best season: spring, summer, fall

Located along the North Umpqua River on one of Oregon's many scenic byways, Susan Creek Falls offers a beautiful, short, cool hike through old-growth Douglas fir and along rock-strewn and moss-lined Susan Creek.

Getting There

From Roseburg travel 28 miles east on OR 138. Just past milepost 28 look for the SUSAN CREEK FALLS trailhead sign and turn left into the parking area.

Special Notes

Wheelchair accessible to the base of Susan Creek Falls. The upper portion of the trail has an abundance of poison oak. No fees or passes are required.

The Trail

The milky, green waters of the North Umpqua River are known to fly-fishermen around the world for their summer run of steelhead trout. Some of the more famous fishermen to try their luck here have included the prolific western writer Zane Grey and actor Clark Gable.

The trailhead is located just to the left of the restrooms at the paved parking area. The well-maintained gravel trail very gradually climbs through moss-covered, old-growth Douglas fir and hemlock. Below the canopy of fir and hemlock grow sword and bracken ferns, rhododendron, salmonberry, Oregon grape, and wild iris. Although you don't see the creek until a few hundred feet before the falls, the trail roughly parallels it

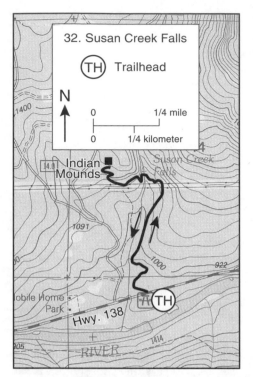

32. Susan Creek Falls

(TH) Trailhead

N

0   1/4 mile
0   1/4 kilometer

Indian Mounds

Susan Creek Falls

1400

1091

1000

922

obile Home Park

Hwy. 138

RIVER

TH

1414

905

for the last ½ mile, and it is always within earshot. The path widens ¼ mile from the trailhead, as it joins an old road, which carries you to where the trail makes a switchback down to the wooden footbridge crossing Susan Creek in front of the falls. Follow the short spur to the right where you can climb atop two large boulders and look down into the splash pool and feel the mist of the falls as it tumbles 60 feet over the moss-lined rock cliff.

Continuing along, the trail steepens and begins to switchback as it climbs for another ½ mile to the Susan Creek Indian Mounds. The now moss-covered piles of rocks are in what was once a spiritual site used by young Native American boys. Here they would spend nights on a vision quest for their guardian spirit. The young boys would fast and conduct the laborious work of stacking the rocks into piles in hopes their vision would be granted.

Susan Creek Falls Trail

If you are up for another short hike, you may want to try the Fall Creek Falls Trail just 4 miles east on OR 138. Just after milepost 34, look for the trailhead sign on the left. The ¾-mile trail begins with a footbridge crossing Fall Creek, lined with birch trees. The trail soon leads through a narrow crack in a very large boulder before gradually climbing the hillside. A short trail forks to the right and leads a few hundred yards to Jobs Garden, a columnar basalt outcrop that is common in the area.

The main trail continues ¼ mile through old-growth Douglas fir, hemlock, and cedar to the base and splash pool of the two-tiered, 50-foot falls.

33

Twin Lakes

Location: Umpqua National Forest

Distance (round-trip): 3¼ miles

Time (round-trip): 2½ hours

Vertical rise: 400 feet

Difficulty: easy

Map: USGS 7½' Twin Lakes Mountain

Best season: spring, summer, fall

Nestled beneath a 300-foot rock bluff and surrounded by Douglas fir and rhododendrons, Twin Lakes makes for a great day hike or an excellent overnight family backpacking destination.

Getting There
From Roseburg follow OR 138 east for 49 miles. Immediately after crossing the North Umpqua (Marster's Bridge), turn right onto the gravel Forest Service Road 4770 (Wilson Creek Road). Follow this road 9 miles to the trailhead parking area.

Special Notes
Bug repellent is essential if you plan on spending the night. No water is available. Check fire restrictions before starting any campfire. No fees or passes are required.

The Trail
The trail begins at the right side of the parking area located at the end of the Wilson Creek Road. You begin by gradually climbing through Douglas fir, western hemlock, red cedar, and a few white fir. After ¼ mile the trail crosses a small, spring-fed creek on a wooden footbridge as it briefly winds past a small older clear-cut area. After another ¼ mile the trail climbs back above the road to a rock outcrop that offers views of Mount Thielsen, Mount Bailey, and the Wilson Creek Road below.

As you continue along the trail, you will notice a surprisingly diverse array of wildflowers mixed among the vine maple, Oregon

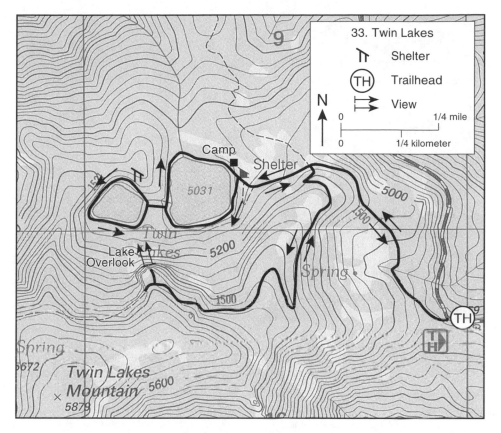

33. Twin Lakes

Ⴑ Shelter

(TH) Trailhead

N ⊢→ View

0   1/4 mile

0   1/4 kilometer

grape, and rhododendron. Spring brings wild iris, columbine, trillium, shootingstar, lady slipper, paintbrush, tiger lily, and helle-bore. After following the trail ¼ mile past the rock outcropping, you arrive at a junction. The trail to the left leads 1¼ miles to the viewpoint overlooking the Twin Lakes. To continue to the lakes, stay to the right where after a few hundred yards you arrive at a second junction. Stay to the right, the trail to the left leads down to an old forest service road after 1¾ miles. After the second junction, a ¼ mile brings you to a boardwalk crossing a small boggy area and the old wood shelter overlooking Large Twin Lake. The large lake covers approximately 14 acres, reaches a depth of 50 feet, and contains some fairly large brook and rainbow trout. The shelter was built in the 1940s by the Forest Service.

If you are spending the night, turn right at the shelter and follow the path where you will find several primitive campsites with fire rings and log tables. Prior to camping, be sure to stop at the ranger station and check the regulations. During the summer months, open fires are strongly discouraged.

To continue on to the smaller lake, turn left and follow the trail that circles the large lake for ¼ mile to a trail leading to the right. Turn right and follow the trail a few hundred yards to the smaller lake, which is less than half the size of its larger twin (6 acres and 30 feet deep) and is a paradise for mosquitoes. Turn

Large Lost Lake

right and follow the trail around the lake to the single campsite and log shelter, which is tucked behind a large boulder, a hundred yards down the trail. The shelter was built in 1995 by the Job Corps. Directly behind the shelter looms the rocky bluff of Twin Lakes Mountain. At the base of the bluff, you'll also find some interesting grotto caves.

Continuing around the loop for ¾ mile brings you back to the large lake. Once you arrive at the large lake, turn left and follow the lakeshore back to the camping area. A right turn will bring you around along the other side of the lake, completing the loop.

If you are spending the night or just want to extend your day hike, turn right at the second junction on your return to the trailhead.

This puts you on the Twin Lakes Mountain Trail, which climbs along the ridgeline through Douglas fir, hemlock, and rhododendron. After hiking 1¼ miles look for a short trail spur on the right. The spur leads to the viewpoint atop the rocky outcrop 300 feet above the lakes. On a clear day the Three Sisters peek above the horizon and the Boulder Creek Wilderness Area.

Although this region of the state has the highest population of mountain lions, count yourself extremely lucky if you get a glimpse of one. More commonly seen are black bears and if you are spending the night, take the proper precautions when storing your food. Also look for deer, elks, herons, hawks, ospreys, and eagles.

34

Toketee Falls

Location: Umpqua National Forest

Distance (round-trip): ¾ mile

Time (round-trip): 45 minutes

Vertical Loss: 100 feet

Difficulty: easy

Map: USGS 7½' Toketee Falls

Best season: spring, summer, fall, winter

While Toketee Falls may be the most picturesque, it is only one of several falls in the area. Two miles east on OR 138 is Watson Falls, which tumbles more than 270 feet over the same basalt flow as Toketee Falls. Continuing east on OR 138, you will soon come across Whitehorse Falls, Clearwater Falls, and Lemolo Falls.

Getting There

From Roseburg travel east 58 miles on OR 138. Just after milepost 58, look for the TOKETEE LAKE/TOKETEE FALLS sign. Turn left onto Toketee–Rigdon Road and follow it approximately ¼ mile where another sign directs you to turn left onto a short gravel road along a wooden diversion pipeline and into the parking lot and picnic area. From Diamond Lake, follow OR 138 west to Toketee-Ridgon road, turn right, and follow the signs to the parking lot.

Special Notes

This lightly used but well-maintained trail utilizes a series of stone and wooden stairs, which can be very slippery in wet and icy conditions. A Northwest Forest Pass is required to park at the trailhead and is available from many private vendors ($5 daily, $30 annually).

The Trail

This secluded treasure of the cascades ranks as one of the most beautiful and unique waterfalls in Oregon. Here the legendary steelhead waters of the North

Toketee Falls

Umpqua River cascades 90 feet over a columnar basalt cliff formed 500,000 years ago when the young Cascades were building nearby Mount Mazama, which later erupted and created Crater Lake. *Toketee* is the Native American word for "pretty" or "beautiful."

The trailhead is located at the small picnic area next to the parking lot. The trail starts with a footbridge crossing a small seasonal stream and then winds its way through 200-foot-tall Douglas fir, hemlock, and western red cedar. In the fall, vine maple adds splashes of yellow and red, which is offset by the green of the conifers.

A little less than ¼ mile from the parking area, the trail meets the North Umpqua River, which makes its way through a jumble of large boulders before entering the gorge that leads to the falls. From here a combination of stone and wooden stairs climb a small rock outcropping along the gorge, with glimpses of the churning water below, and begins a gradual decent to the observation platform. The tree house–like platform, which is built around two Douglas firs and a yew tree, hangs over the gorge and offers a beautiful view of the falls looking down through cedar and fir.

On the return trip take some time to look for American dippers, which frequent the water above the gorge. They are easily recognized by their upturned tails and constant "dipping" motion. In search of the aquatic insects on which they feed, these remarkable little brown birds either dive or walk directly into the swift current and precariously walk along the bottom by grabbing onto stones.

Located just 2¼ miles east of Toketee Falls on OR 138 is the spectacular 270-foot-high Watson Falls. From Toketee Falls travel east 2¼ miles on OR 138 to Fish

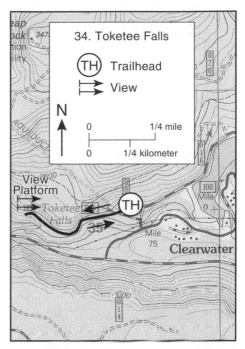

Creek road and look for the Watson Falls Sign. Turn right onto Fish Creek Road, follow it ¼ mile, and turn right into the Watson Falls parking area.

The trail begins at the right side of the parking area and after crossing Fish Creek Road loosely follows Watson Creek upstream as it tumbles over moss-covered rocks and logs. After a gradual climb of a little less than ¼ mile, the trail crosses Watson Creek on a long wooden boardwalk and then arrives at a junction. Turn left and follow the trail a few hundred yards to the base of the third highest waterfall in the state. Here the waters of Watson Creek make a dramatic single plunge over the 500,000-year-old basalt cliff. On your return trip, stay to the left, passing the boardwalk, and follow the trail ¼ mile through Douglas fir and cedar back down to Fish Creek Road. From here follow the road to the right back to the parking area.

35

Mount Thielsen

Location: Mount Thielsen Wilderness Area

Distance (round-trip): 10 miles

Time (round-trip): 6 hours

Vertical gain: 3,800 feet

Difficulty: difficult

Maps: USGS 7½' Mount Thielsen; USFS Mount Thielsen Wilderness Area

Best season: summer, early fall

One of the most recognizable peaks in the Cascades, Mount Thielsen's 100,000-year-old weathered spire stands 9,182 feet above the surrounding landscape and offers incredible views of Diamond Lake, Mount Bailey, the Three Sisters, and the rim of Crater Lake.

Getting There

From Roseburg travel east 82 miles on OR 138 and look for the THIELSEN TRAILHEAD sign on the left. From Medford drive 81 miles east on OR 62 and OR 230 to the intersection of OR 138. Turn west on OR 138 and after 1½ miles look for the THIELSEN TRAILHEAD sign on the right.

Special Notes

The final few hundred feet to the summit is hazardous and should not be attempted without the proper climbing experience and equipment. The "Lightning Rod of the Cascades" is a well-deserved nickname, and a hasty retreat is strongly advised with the onset of bad weather. A Northwest Forest Pass is required to park at the trailhead and is available from many private vendors ($5 daily, $30 annually).

The Trail

More than 250,000 years ago, the weathered and jagged peak of Mount Thielsen was once the core of an active, 11,000-foot shield volcano composed of basalt andesite. A little more than 100,000 years ago, volcanic activity ceased and Ice Age

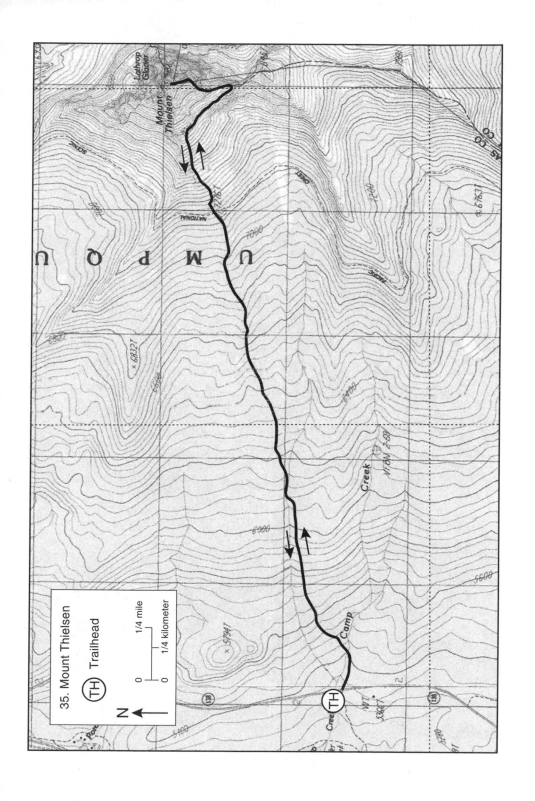

35. Mount Thielsen

(TH) Trailhead

N

0   1/4 mile

0   1/4 kilometer

Mount Thielsen

glaciers carved away the once-gentle slopes.

From the trailhead, located on the left end of the large, paved parking area, you begin by gradually climbing a ridge through lodgepole pine, mountain hemlock, and huckleberry. The trail is composed of pumice and ash from the eruption of Mount Mazama, which occurred 7,700 years ago, and some of these deposits are more than 60 feet deep. After approximately 1 ½ miles, you come to a trail junction with the Spruce Ridge Trail, which leads 2½ miles to the Howlock Mountain Trail. Stay to the right to continue up Mount Thielsen where after another ½ mile a small sign tells you that you have crossed into the 55,100-acre Mount Thielsen Wilderness Area. As you continue on another 2 miles, the trail takes you up and over a small ridge, with great views of the mountain ahead, and brings you to the intersection of the Pacific Crest Trail (PCT).

This famed trail stretches 2,655 miles from the border of Mexico to the border of Canada, passing through California, Oregon, and Washington. Along the way the trail passes through 7 national parks, 24 national forests, and 33 national wilderness areas. The idea of a border-to-border trail was conceived in 1932; however, the trail was not completed until 1993. While thousands of people enjoy portions of the trail each year, it is an interesting bit of trivia that more people have climbed Mount Everest than have hiked the entire length of the PCT.

From the intersection of the PCT, continue straight along a steep secondary trail that leads up the crest of the ridge. As you continue to climb to the tree line, lodgepole pine soon gives way to white bark pine and, in the spring, a mixture of paintbrush and penstemon. The footing also becomes less secure as the rocky trail turns to scree. Keep right along the poorly defined trail as it passes along the ridge and around the eastern side of the summit peak to the small ledge overlooking Thielsen Creek, which appears as a tiny silver ribbon more than 1,500 feet below. I recommend turning around here. From this point the challenging hike turns into mountaineering, and a climb up the summit should not be attempted without the proper climbing experience and equipment.

To the south lie Diamond Lake, Mount Bailey, and the rim of Crater Lake. To the north lie Tipsoo Peak and the Three Sisters. *Fulgerite* (a glassy black coating of recrystallized rock) is abundant on the peak and attests to the frequency of lightning strikes.

Jays, hawks, and eagles populate the area as do elk, mule deer, coyote, bobcat, black bear, and the ever-elusive mountain lion.

36

Crater Lake

Location: Crater Lake National Park

Distance (round-trip): 1–5 miles

Time (round-trip): ¾–5 hours

Vertical rise: 100–1,400 feet

Difficulty: easy–moderate

Maps: USGS 7½' Crater Lake West, Crater Lake Eas;, Crater Lake National Park map and brochure

Best season: spring, summer, fall

In 1902, President Theodore Roosevelt signed legislation creating Oregon's only national park, Crater Lake, and the nation's fifth national park. Its hypnotic blue waters, a result of its great depth and clarity, belie the cataclysmic forces that created the lake 7,500 years ago. This chapter describes three easy-to-moderate hikes that explore various areas of this unique park.

Getting There

From Roseburg drive east 76 miles on OR 138 to the junction of US 230. Turn left and continue on OR 138 for 5 miles to the entrance of Crater Lake National Park on your right.

Special Notes

The north entrance and Rim Drive are usually closed due to snow between October and May. A $10 entrance fee, good for seven days, is required at the entrance gates.

The Trail

Mount Mazama began to rise approximately 400,000 years ago as highly complex stratovolcano. Composed of a series of eroded cones, it reached an eventual height of about 12,000 feet. Mazama began a series of large eruptions 7,700 years ago, ejecting almost 13 cubic miles of thick, rhyodacite lava, which formed Llao Rock and the formations around Cleetwood Cove. The eruption of the rhyodacite released the pressure contained in the volcano's magma chamber, resulting in a cataclysmic explosive eruption

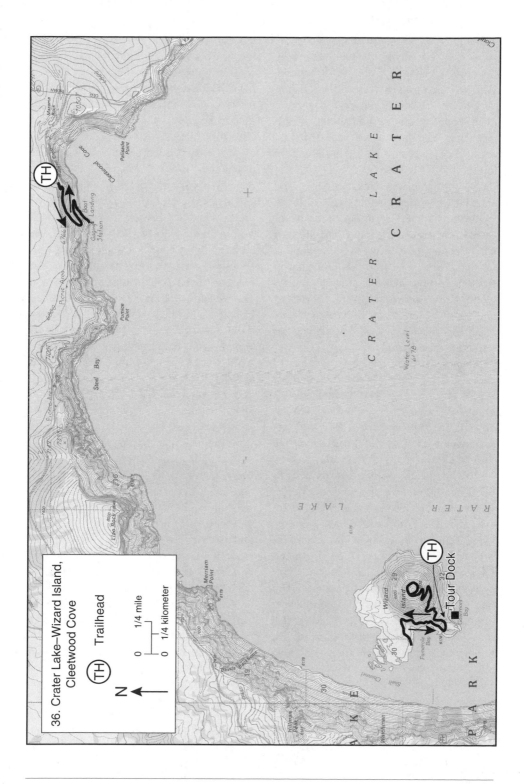

36. Crater Lake–Wizard Island, Cleetwood Cove

(TH) Trailhead

N

0   1/4 mile
0   1/4 kilometer

ejecting 13 cubic miles of the mountain, more than two hundred times greater than the 1980 eruption of Mount St. Helens. With so much material removed, the mountain could no longer support itself and collapsed inward, creating the 4,000-foot-deep *caldera* (a large, basin-shaped volcanic depression, more or less circular in form).

As the eruptions subsided, rain and snowmelt gradually filled the caldera. Today its depth is 1,958 feet, making it the deepest lake in the United States and the seventh deepest lake in the world. Although Crater Lake receives an annual precipitation of 66 inches per year—the equivalent of 44 feet of that as snow—the lake is not getting any deeper. Evaporation and seepage balance the incoming flow, maintaining its depth to within 3 feet.

One of the most distinctive features of Crater Lake is Wizard Island. Shortly after Mount Mazama collapsed, several smaller eruptions created two cinder cones in the caldera. The Merriam cone still lies 480 feet beneath the water, while Wizard Island rises 750 feet above the lake's surface.

This moderate 4¾-mile hike is actually two hikes with a very pleasant boat ride in between. It also follows the only trail to access the clear waters of the lake. From the lodge, drive 10½ miles north (clockwise around the lake) to the well-marked Cleetwood Cove parking area.

Although it may not seem necessary, you may want to consider bringing along a light jacket or sweatshirt as the boat ride can be quite cool. The trailhead is located just across the Rim Drive from the parking area and immediately begins to switchback down the caldera wall. The trail passes through moss-covered lodgepole pine, red fir, and mountain hemlock. Along the way countless vistas greet you as you look down the rim and through the trees to the lake below. This is a very busy trail during the summer months, so be prepared to greet a number of people along the 1-mile route to the lake. You may also share the trail with golden-mantled ground squirrels and Clark's nutcrackers.

At the dock, boats arrive and depart approximately every 45 minutes. However, during the summer months you may have to wait a bit longer due to the increased tourist traffic. From Cleetwood Cove it's a 45-minute boat ride to Wizard Island. The view from the boat provides an entirely new perspective concerning the magnitude of the eruption that formed the sizable lake. On your way to the island, you will pass below Llao Rock, which stands approximately 2,000 feet above the surface of the lake, or approximately the same as the deepest part of the lake. As you disembark from the boat at Wizard Island, you will be given a numbered pass, which will determine your priority for the return trip, as well as ensure that no one is left on the island overnight. There is no overnight camping on the island.

From the dock follow the well-marked trail a few hundred yards to the first junction. The left path leads ¼ mile to the emerald waters of Fumarole Bay. The right fork switchbacks 1 mile through Shasta red fir and up the flanks of the cinder cone. As you reach the summit, you can turn either right or left to follow the short loop around the 90-foot-deep summit crater.

Although fish are not native to the lake, early explorers introduced various species of trout and kokanee (landlocked salmon). Fishing from the island is not only permitted but is actually encouraged. No license is needed; the only requirement is that you do not use bait.

The return boat trip takes about an hour and fifteen minutes and follows the south

Pinnacles seen from Godfrey Glen Nature Trail

shore. Along the way, the boat passes by the Phantom Ship, a rock island rising 167 feet above the surface of the lake and formed during the creation of Mount Mazama; it is also one of the oldest formations in the park. If you're lucky, the boat may also pass by the Old Man of the Lake, a floating log that has been a resident of the lake for more than a century. From the boat dock at Cleetwood Cove, it's a steep 1-mile climb of 650 feet back up the caldera wall to the parking area.

Mount Scott is the highest point in the park and one of the oldest formations, dating back 400,000 years. It once stood on the flanks of the much larger Mount Manama and is the second of our Crater Lake hikes. The trailhead for the moderate 5-mile climb to the summit is located on the far east side of the lake. From the lodge travel south (counterclockwise) 15 miles, along the Rim Drive to the wide parking area on the right.

The trail begins its 1,000-foot climb along an old service road. As it wraps around to the south side, it passes through a shallow glacial depression, groves of white bark pine, and meadows of spring wildflowers, such as paintbrush and penstemon. After following the trail for ½ mile, it begins to gradually steepen. Another mile along the trail brings you to a series of long switchbacks as you climb to the summit. The majority of the trail is composed of pumice gravel, remnants of Mount Manama's eruption. However, in contrast to much of the park, many of the rocky outcroppings on the south side escaped the destruction of the Mazama eruption and have been polished by glaciers of the last Ice Age. Along the way, the ever-persistent Clark's nutcracker will keep you company.

At the 8,929-foot summit, you will be greeted by a lookout that was built in 1952 by the National Park Service that offers an amazing panoramic view of the lake. To the north, look for Mount Thielsen and the Three Sisters. To the south lie the Sky Lakes Wilderness Area, Klamath Lake, Mount McLaughlin, and the snowy tip of Mount Shasta.

The third hike of Crater Lake explores the often-overlooked Godfrey Glen Nature Trail, which is located 1½ miles east of the Mazama Village Campground. From the parking area, the level, mile-long trail immediately forks. Stay to the left where the trail soon joins the rim of the Godfrey Glen created by Munson Creek. At the ¼-mile mark, you are treated to a view of the glen and the steep canyon walls. The surrounding canyon walls are composed of ash and pumice from the final eruptions of Mount Mazama. The oddly shaped "pinnacles" along the canyon walls are the remnants of fumaroles formed when the ash and pumice flows trapped super-heated gases. As the gases made their way to the surface, a chimneylike structure was formed by the welding together of the surrounding material. Over the past 7,000 years, the elements and Munson Creek have washed away the softer and looser material leaving the hollow reminders of Mazama's past. From here you can also hear the 70-foot-high Duwee Falls, as the waters of Munson Creek fall into the glen.

Another ½ mile brings you to a viewpoint overlooking the lush valley floor below, populated by hemlock and summer wildflowers. The trail continues along the canyon rim for another ¼ mile before crossing over to Annie Creek Canyon and then back to the parking area.

Although Crater Lake is visited by more than a quarter-million people each year, the majority stay near the lake or the other viewpoints. This makes the backcountry surrounding the lake some of the most underused and unspoiled in the Cascades. Rich in wildlife, Crater Lake's backcountry fauna includes mountain lion, black bear, fox, elk, deer, porcupine, squirrel, pika, and martin.

IV

High Desert

Fort Rock Church

The southeastern portion of the state has much in common with the Great Basin region of Idaho, Nevada, Utah, and Wyoming. Broad, wide basins with an average elevation above 4,000 feet separate fault-block mountains, which, like Steens Mountain, can reach a height of nearly 10,000 feet. The southeast is also the least populated region in Oregon, with a population density of less than one person per square mile, comparable to that of Alaska.

In the north the high desert is punctuated by several mountain ranges, which include the Ochoco, Aldrich, Strawberry, and the Elkhorn; together they're called the Blue Mountains. The peaks in these mountains range in height from 7,000 to 9,000 feet.

Tucked away in the northeastern corner is perhaps the state's most spectacular scenery. Along the border with Idaho lies Hell's Canyon, North America's deepest canyon. You can't help but feel exceptionally small as you stand on the edge and look across the endless ridges. Just a few miles to the south of Hell's Canyon lie the Wallowa Mountains. Nicknamed the "Alps of Oregon," the Wallowas are much more aligned geologically with the Rockies than the volcanic peaks of the Cascades. The granite and marble peaks of the Wallowas reach a height of nearly 10,000 feet and contain more than 500 miles of hiking trails. They are also home to the 385,541-acre Eagle Cap Wilderness Area, Oregon's largest.

Climate

The climate of the southeast portion of the state is very dry; many places experience an annual rainfall of less than 10 inches, with most of this precipitation occurring in winter. It is also a land of extreme daily and seasonal temperature ranges. Winter temperatures can hover near or below freezing for weeks, while in summer temperatures can easily reach well above 100 degrees.

The climate to the north is more varied than that of the southeast and can fluctuate to an even greater degree per day, regardless of season. The region has recorded both the highest and lowest temperatures in the state—119 degrees in Pendleton and −54 degrees in Seneca, respectively. Annual precipitation ranges from less than 10 inches in the dryer valleys to as much as 60 inches in the Wallowa Mountains.

Trails in the lower elevations are usually open all year. The upper trails of Steens Mountain are typically open from the end of May to October. Trails in the Wallowa Mountains clear by mid-June and are open until September, although fallen snow around some of the high alpine lakes can linger well into August. In the highest elevations, snow is possible year-round.

Precautions

When hiking at high elevations, it is important to carry extra water, and sunscreen and to take your time. When hiking in the desert, it is a good idea to triple the amount of water you typically carry.

Although black bears and mountain lions reside in the area, they are very shy and usually avoid any contact with humans. However, when camping in the wilderness it is wise to store food away from tents.

In the southeastern portion of the state, the availability of gasoline may be a concern. It is not uncommon to make a round-trip of more than 200 miles without encountering a service station. If you are planning a long trip, make sure your tank is full and consider carrying extra fuel.

Much of eastern Oregon is classified as open range. Use caution when you see the yellow OPEN RANGE or LIVESTOCK road signs, and remember that if you are involved in an accident, not only will you be responsible for the repairs to your car, but you are also liable for the value of, or injuries to, the animal.

Attractions

The Malheur National Wildlife Refuge is located 37 miles south of Burns and is one of Oregon's true wonders. The refuge has more than 187,000 acres of wetlands, riparian areas, meadows, and sagebrush and juniper uplands. More than 320 species of birds, 58 species of mammals, and 10 species of fish, all native to the region, can be found in the refuge during the year. More than 130 species of birds nest on the refuge. Sandhill cranes, egrets, heron, ibis, pelicans, avocets, coots, grebes, swans, and numerous ducks and songbirds are common sights within the refuge, as are mule deer and pronghorn antelope.

Located 3½ miles south of Bend on US 97, the High Desert Museum offers self-guided tours of exhibits and presentations featuring the region's history, culture, arts, and wildlife. The museum also includes a small collection of native animals in their natural habitat.

The John Day Fossil Beds National Monument is divided into three units: the Painted Hills Unit, northwest of Mitchell; the Clarno Unit, 20 miles west of Fossil; and the Sheep Rock Unit, located northwest of Dayville. The Sheep Rock Unit is also the location of the visitor center, which is open daily, March through October. The center has wonderful displays of the fossils discovered in the monument. The U.S. Congress established the John Day Fossil Beds National Monument in 1975. Its three units encompass 14,000 acres. Each of the units offers short interpretive trails that explore the sedimentary rocks that preserve a 40-million-year record of plant and animal life during the Cenozoic era (called the "Age of Mammals and Flowering Plants" by geologists).

Traveling 24 miles north of Imnaha, along a steep, winding, gravel road, brings you to the awe-inspiring Hat Point Overlook. At an elevation of 6,982 feet, the overlook is perched on the western edge of Hells Canyon and overlooks the deepest gorge in North America. The thin ribbon of the Snake River winds its way through the canyon more than 5,700 feet below the overlook with Idaho's 9,000-foot-high Seven Devils Mountains, visible in the distance.

37

Mount Howard Summit Loop

Location: 6 miles south of Joseph

Distance (round-trip): 5½ miles

Time (round-trip): 4 hours

Vertical rise: 1,100 feet

Difficulty: moderate

Map: USGS 7½' Mount Howard

Best season: spring, summer, fall

After an enjoyable tram ride up to the summit of Mount Howard, you can choose to stroll around the summit loop, hike to East Peak, or simply have lunch at the Summit Café and enjoy the company of some extremely chubby Columbian ground squirrels.

Getting There
From La Grande follow OR 82 for 75 miles through Enterprise to Joseph. From Joseph follow the state park signs another 6 miles along the eastern shore of Wallowa Lake. The tramway station is located just ¼ mile past the park entrance on the left.

Special Notes
Depending on the weather, the tramway operates between the months of May and September from 10 AM to 5 PM with the last tram down leaving at 5:45 PM. A round-trip costs $19.

The Trail
When it was built in 1970, the Mount Howard tramway was the tallest in the North America. Today it remains the steepest, climbing 3,500 feet in just over 3 miles. After an exhilarating ride up the side of the mountain, you exit the tram car onto the patio of the Summit Café. From the café follow the well-traveled path to the right for a ¼ mile where the trail takes you through clusters of white bark pine and up a short set of stairs to the Royal Purple Overlook. From here you can look across Wallowa Lake to Chief Joseph Mountain, while a little

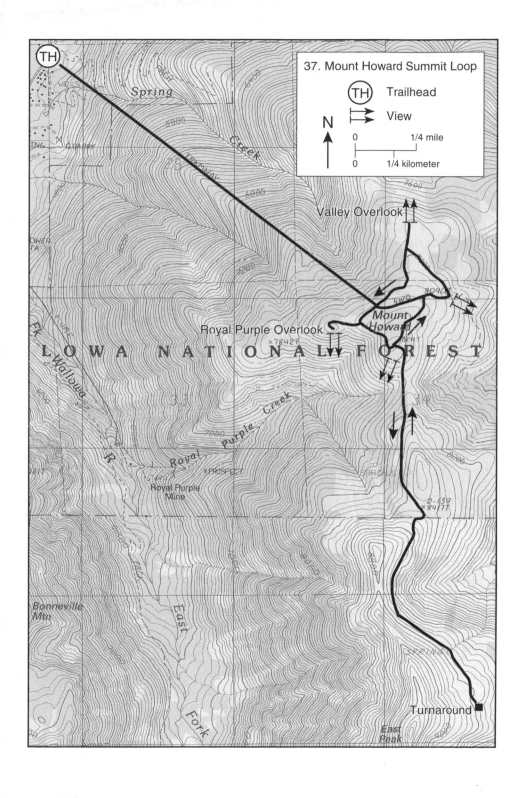

TH Trailhead

N   View

0   1/4 mile
0   1/4 kilometer

Spring

Creek

Valley Overlook

Mount
Howard

Royal Purple Overlook

L O W A   N A T I O N A L   F O R E S T

Royal   Purple   Creek

L. Wallowa

Royal

R

PROSPECT

Royal Purple
Mine

East

Bonneville
Mtn

Fork

Turnaround

East
Peak

Wallowa Range from Mount Howard

farther south lie the Matterhorn and Eagle Cap, the wilderness area's namesake peak.

From the Royal Purple Overlook, backtrack down the steps and stay to the right at the junction. The trail makes a few short switchbacks up to the 8,240-foot-high summit of Mount Howard a little less than a ½ mile away. The views from the summit include Hells Canyon and Zumwalt Prairie, a 200-square-mile remnant grassland to the east and the heart of the Wallowa's granite peaks to the west.

From the summit turn right at the junction atop the Mount Howard Summit and follow the lightly used trail ¼ mile down to a small saddle. From here the trail steepens as it climbs the adjacent ridge. After another ¾ mile you arrive at a small meadow nourished by springs just below the trail. Monkeyflowers, lupines, gentians, and a few lilies can be found in the early summer.

From here the trail passes through the meadow and begins a steep climb for another ¼ mile before leveling off as it wraps around 9,380-foot-high East Peak where you officially cross the boundary into the Eagle Cap Wilderness area. Continuing on for another ¾ mile brings you to a spring-fed meadow of wildflowers on the east side of the peak. The view extends over the McCully Basin below to Hells Canyon and the Seven Devils Mountains in Idaho.

After backtracking to the summit loop trail, turn right where, after another ¼ mile, you reach a junction. The path to the left leads back to the café and tram station. Stay to the right to continue along the main trail where you encounter a short trail spur to the right. Following the trail for a ½ mile brings you to the Valley Overlook. As the name implies, this overlook offers a beautiful view of the blue waters of Wallowa Lake and surrounding ranch and farmland of the valley. From the overlook, it's just a ½ mile back to the café and tramway station.

38

BC Creek Falls

Location: Wallowa Lake State Park

Distance (round-trip): 2¾ miles

Time (round-trip): 2 hours

Vertical rise: 400 feet

Difficulty: easy

Map: USGS 7½' Mount Howard

Best season: spring, summer, fall

This short but enjoyable trail passes along the West Fork of the Wallowa River and then climbs up to meet the Double Falls on BC Creek.

Getting There

From La Grande follow OR 82 for 75 miles through Enterprise to Joseph. From Joseph follow the state park signs another 6 miles along the eastern shore of Wallowa Lake. Pass by the tramway station and continue ¼ mile to the road's end. The Wallowa Lake trailhead is located on the left next to the power station.

Special Notes

The trail can become quite crowded during the spring and summer due to its proximity to the resort and campground. Be prepared to share the trail with a horse or two on the lower section of the trail. There are several steep drop-offs along the trail and care should be taken when hiking with small children. No permits or access fees are required.

The Trail

The trailhead is located just ¼ mile up the road from the parking area of the Mount Howard tramway. The trail begins by meandering past the information board listing the current regulations and then passes behind the small power plant located at the end of the road. The trail shares the trailhead with the Aneroid Lake Trail, which forks off to the left. Instead, stay to the right as the trail climbs over and around moss-covered

Wallowa River from trail bridge

rocks and through stands of fir and aspen. After a ¼ mile you will encounter a second fork. The left fork leads to Ice Lake after a steep 7½-mile hike. Follow the CHIEF JOSEPH TRAIL sign along the right fork where the trail soon runs along the rim of the 100-foot-deep gorge, which was carved by the West Fork of the Wallowa River as it cuts its way through to Wallowa Lake. A faint trail spur to the right leading a few hundred yards along the gorge and down to a rock outcrop offers a wonderful view of the river as it passes through the gorge.

Following the trail for another ¼ mile past the Ice Lake Trail junction brings you to a footbridge that crosses the clear, cold waters of the Wallowa river. If you take some time and pause at the bridge you may also get a chance to see see American dippers feeding beneath the waters of the river. From the base of the bridge the trail begins a series of steep switchbacks that leads up a small boulder field that offers views of the

Wallowa river below. The trail gradually levels off as it passes through stands of Douglas fir and western larch, where before long you come to a nice, cliff-side viewpoint overlooking the south end of Wallowa Lake and the campground, with Mount Howard and its tram above.

Along the way you will be accompanied by chipmunks, ground squirrels, and perhaps a pika chirping at you from its hiding place among the rocks. Downy woodpeckers and jays also populate the forest. Shootingstars and paintbrushes can also be found along the trail. From the viewpoint. it's an easy, level ¼ mile to the bridge that crosses between the 40-foot-high upper and lower falls on BC Creek. From the falls retrace your steps back down to the trailhead.

The trail continues past the falls above the lake where it eventually begins a series of long switchbacks up the side of Chief Joseph Mountain for a very strenuous 6¼ miles.

For those looking for a place to spend the night, Wallowa Lake State Park, located on the south end of the lake, offers 121 full-service sites for RVs, 89 primitive tent sites, 2 yurts, and a cabin. Fees range from $13 to $58 a night. The park is popular and reservations are recommended in the busy summer months.

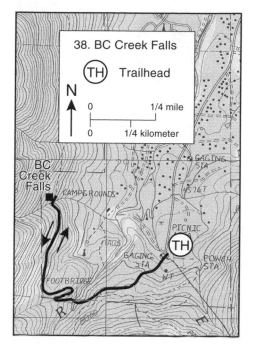

39

Eagle Cap

Location: Eagle Cap Wilderness Area

Distance (round-trip): 14¾ miles,
19¾ miles

Time (round-trip): 10 hours, overnight

Vertical gain: 2,000 feet, 4,000 feet

Difficulty: difficult, very difficult

Map: USGS 7½' Steamboat Lake, Eagle Cap

Best season: late spring, summer, early fall

This trail provides a wonderful opportunity to sample the Eagle Cap experience. It follows the pure and clear waters of the Lostine River through lodgepole pine and alpine meadows to an alpine lake nestled in a glacial moraine below the wilderness's namesake peak.

Getting There

From La Grande follow OR 82 north 55 miles, following the signs toward Enterprise and Wallowa Lake. From Lostine, turn right onto the Lostine River Road, following the signs marked LOSTINE RIVER CAMPGROUNDS. The road loosely parallels the river for 12 paved miles followed by 6 gravel/dirt miles to its end at the Two Pan trailhead. The Eagle Cap trailhead is located just past the message board.

Special Notes

If you intend to camp at Mirror Lake, make sure to be prepared for a variety of weather conditions. Weather can change very rapidly and snow is possible year-round.

Camping is prohibited within 100 feet of the lake, and campfires, when permitted in the wilderness area, are prohibited within ¼ mile of the lake.

A Northwest Forest Pass is required to park at the trailhead and is available at ranger stations and from many private vendors ($5 daily, $30 annually).

The Trail

The trailhead is located just to the right of the information board. A few hundred yards

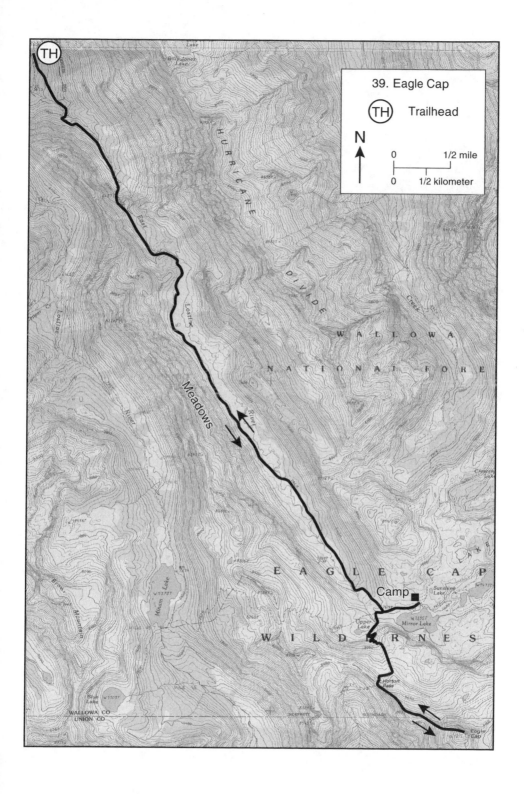

39. Eagle Cap

(TH) Trailhead

N

0   1/2 mile
0   1/2 kilometer

Lostine River

past the trailhead, the trail forks. The right fork follows the West Fork of the Lostine River; stay to the left and follow the East Fork of the Lostine River Trail. After following the trail for ¾ mile through spruce and lodgepole pine, you enter the Eagle Cap Wilderness Area and join the river near a small, picturesque waterfall where the trail crosses the river on a small footbridge.

From here the trail steepens as it begins to climb through a series of short switchbacks. Over the next 2 miles you climb more than 1,300 feet before coming to a small series of ponds at the north end of Lostine Meadows. As you climb you may hear the shrill little chirps of pikas as they scurry about the rocks.

The next 2½ miles are essentially level as the trail follows the river as it meanders through the meadow. Fir and pine trees cluster here for protection, creating meadows that fill with wildflowers such as paintbrush, lupine, gentian, tiger lily, and avalanche lily in the late spring. The meadows are also home to ground squirrels and mule deer. For those heading on to the summit of Eagle Cap, the distant peak is beautifully framed by the valley walls and the meadow's wildflowers.

Near the south end of the meadows, the trail crosses the river and begins a gradual climb. It continues above the valley through fir and pine for another 1½ miles to where it steepens as it passes through a series of short switchbacks. After climbing a ½ mile, a trail junction overlooks the alpine Mirror Lake. Here the glacial origin of the region is evident as polished granite boulders abound.

Turn left and go a few hundred yards to the cold waters of Mirror Lake. Early in the morning, when the water is like glass, the reflection of Eagle Cap provides a wonderful photo opportunity and illustrates how the lake got its name. If you plan on spending the night, Mirror Lake is an excellent campsite.

If you are continuing to the summit from the trail junction just above the lake, continue straight and then stay to the left at the next two junctions, which are located, respectively, 1 mile and 1½ miles ahead. The summit is 1¼ miles past and 1,000 feet above the last junction. As you continue to gain elevation along the exposed trail the white bark pines become smaller and more contorted and the views become more and more impressive. At the 9,570-foot summit, you can peer over the cliff and down onto Glacier Lake, 1,500 feet below. To the north lie the Matterhorn and Saoagawea. Marble Mountain lies to the southeast. A little more to the west, over Mirror Lake, lie the Lostine River valley and your route back to Two Pan.

Along the way you may encounter Rocky Mountain elk, and black bears. Bighorn sheep and mountain goats also populate the Wallowas; however, due to the trail's popularity, count yourself lucky if you catch a glimpse of either.

40

Hurricane Creek/Echo Lake

Location: Eagle Cap Wilderness Area

Distance (round-trip): 10 miles, 15½ miles

Time (round-trip): 8 hours, overnight

Vertical gain: 1,000 feet, 3,400 feet

Difficulty: moderate, difficult

Map: USGS 7½' Chief Joseph Mountain, Eagle Cap

Best season: spring, summer, fall

This hike up the steep and narrow canyon offers either a moderate day hike along the crystal-clear waters of Hurricane Creek or an overnight camping trip to the alpine wonders of Echo Lake.

Getting There

From La Grande follow OR 82 north 65 miles to Enterprise. Turn right onto Hurricane Creek Road and follow it 9 miles, following the HURRICANE CREEK signs to the roads end at the trailhead parking area.

Special Notes

If you intend to camp at Echo Lake, be prepared for a variety of weather conditions. Weather can change very rapidly and snow is possible year-round.

Camping is prohibited within 100 feet of the lake, and campfires, when permitted in the wilderness area, are prohibited within ¼ mile of the lake.

A Northwest Forest Pass is required to park at the trailhead and is available at ranger stations and from many private vendors ($5 daily, $30 annually).

The Trail

The trailhead is located on the south end of the parking area opposite the horse-loading area. The trail begins by passing through a small grove of aspen and lodgepole pine. Just a hundred yards from the trailhead, you arrive at a junction with the LeGore Lake Trail. Take the right trail and follow the LeGore Lake Trail for a short ¼ mile, which will bring you to the edge of

Falls Creek Falls

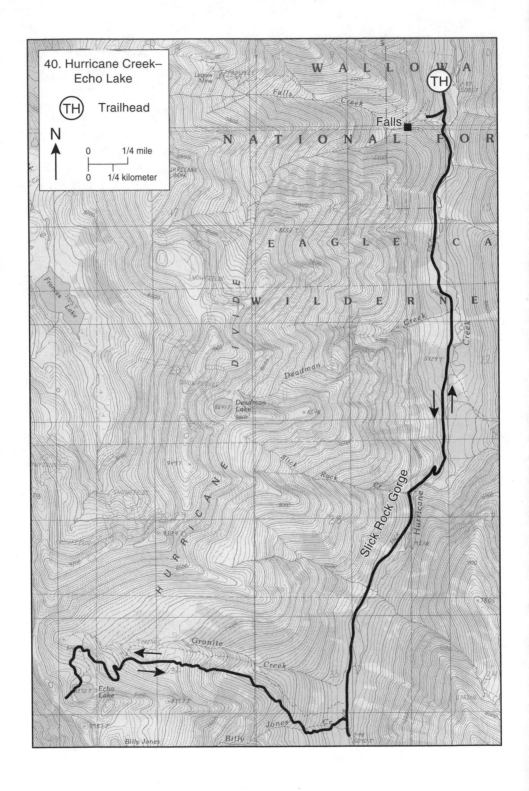

40. Hurricane Creek–
Echo Lake

(TH) Trailhead

N

0   1/4 mile
0   1/4 kilometer

WALLOWA

TH

Falls

NATIONAL FOR

EAGLE CA

DIVIDE WILDERNE

Deadman

Deadman
Lake

Slick Rock

Hurricane

Slick Rock Gorge

HURRICANE

Granite

Creek

Echo
Lake

Jones Cr.

Billy Jones   Billy

Frances Lake

Falls Creek and give you a great view of Falls Creek Falls. The falls tumbles over the barren rock face that has been scoured clean by spring floods and winter avalanches. Snowcapped Sawtooth Peak and Twin Peak are high in the distance. From here the LeGore trail continues for another very steep and very strenuous 3¾ mile, past an old mine and on to the alpine LeGore Lake. However, to continue on along Hurricane Creek, after viewing the falls, retrace your steps and turn right at the junction. After you rejoin the trail, it is only a few hundred more yards to where you pass through the boulder-strewn avalanche chute and ford Falls Creek.

After crossing Falls Creek, and as you continue your hike along the creek, you begin to notice the many barren channels that have been carved down the steep canyon walls. The majority have been formed by avalanches during the winter. Not only does this attest to their awesome power, but they also serve as a warning to the winter traveler.

A small sign marks the boundary of the Eagle Cap Wilderness as you gradually climb 1½ miles along the creek where you soon arrive at the boulder field of Deadman Creek. Here again, the trail makes its way through the run-out of an avalanche and flood chute where you ford the small creek.

After another 1½ miles, the trail makes a short climb through a couple of switchbacks up to Slick Rock Gorge. Here the waters of Hurricane Creek and Slick Rock Creek combine and carve a dramatic 200-foot-deep slot through the rock. The trail crosses the scoured rock canyon of Slick Rock Creek just above the confluence with Hurricane Creek.

Traveling along for another 1½ miles through fir and the occasional juniper brings you to the junction for Echo Lake. If you have planned on just a day hike, stay to the left and continue along the creek for another ¼ mile to the small meadow where the trail crosses Hurricane Creek. Wildflowers in the meadow include paintbrush, lilies, and a few wild irises. Turn back here to complete an 8¼-mile moderate hike.

For those who are a bit more adventurous and in shape, turn right and begin the climb to Echo Lake. From here the trail becomes much more difficult as it climbs over 2,300 feet in 3 miles. For the first ½ mile, the trail climbs the ridgeline between Granite Creek and Billy Jones Creek before veering north to Granite Creek, which it follows up and over the rim of the steep Hurricane Creek Canyon. As you continue on a little farther, you reach a small pond on your left, which makes for a good spot to rest before continuing on the remaining 1 mile to the lake. After several more switchbacks, you begin to enter the alpine region and finally come to the clear, clean waters of Echo Lake. The lake is tucked just below Hurricane Divide and nestled in an east-facing glacial moraine. At an elevation of more than 8,300 feet, you're likely to encounter snow—regardless of the season—so be prepared for all kinds of weather.

Wildlife in the area includes Columbian ground squirrels, marmots, bighorn sheep, and the occasional black bear. The chirping of pika can be heard in the rocks next to the lake as they dry their food in the sun in preparation for winter, which, up here, is never far away.

41

Eureka Point

Location: Hells Canyon Recreation Area

Distance (round-trip): 7¼ miles

Time (round-trip): 5 hours

Vertical rise: 1,800 feet

Difficulty: moderate

Map: USGS 7½' Eureka

Best season: spring, fall

At its deepest point, Hells Canyon is nearly 8,000 feet deep, making it the deepest canyon in North America, surpassing even the Grand Canyon.

Getting There

From La Grande follow OR 82 north 65 miles to Enterprise. Continue on OR 82 through Enterprise another 3½ miles to Crow Creek Road and turn left. Follow Crow Creek Road 4¼ miles to Zumwalt Road and turn right. The first 2 miles are paved; it then turns into a very well maintained gravel road. Follow Zumwalt Road approximately 32 miles to Forest Service Road 780 and turn right, following the BUCKHORN LOOKOUT signs. Follow Forest Service Road 780, ½ mile to the lookout.

Special Notes

Summer temperatures, especially in the lower elevations of the canyon, can easily exceed 100 degrees Fahrenheit. Bring plenty of water and dress appropriately.

Although somewhat scarce, rattlesnakes do inhabit the area. Care should be taken when stepping over rocks or hidden areas. When passing through gates and fences, be sure to leave them open or closed as you found them. No fees or permits are required.

The Trail

On your drive in to the trailhead you pass through the Zumwalt Prairie. This 42-square-mile site was purchased by The

Abandoned homestead on the Zumwalt Prairie

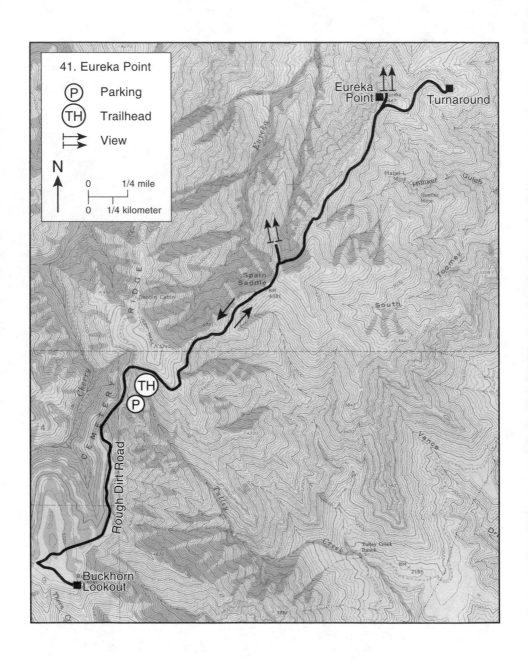

41. Eureka Point

P   Parking

TH   Trailhead

⇉   View

N

| 0 | 1/4 mile |
| 0 | 1/4 kilometer |

Eureka Point

Turnaround

Spain Saddle

TH

P

Rough Dirt Road

CEMETERY RIDGE

Buckhorn Lookout

Nature Conservancy in 2000 and is part of North America's largest remaining expanse of native bunchgrass prairie. The preserve is also home to one of the largest known concentrations of breeding hawks and eagles in North America. Ferruginous hawks and Swainson's hawks, along with golden eagles, red-tailed hawks, rough-legged hawks, and prairie falcons, all reside on the preserve. The drive in also offers an opportunity to photograph a few of the old, abandoned homesteads with the backdrop of the Seven Devils or Wallowa Mountains.

After passing through the prairie, the road winds through a ponderosa pine forest and along the rim of the canyon to the Buckhorn Lookout. Built in the early 1930s, the lookout was staffed until recently, when technology eliminated any need for human resources. At an elevation of 5,300 feet, it sits a little more than 4,300 feet above the Snake and Imnaha Rivers, which are hidden in the maze of canyons below. Looking southwest over Hat Point are the 9,000-foot-high Seven Devils Mountains of Idaho.

The canyon began its formation approximately 300 million years ago with a series of volcanic eruptions on what was then a series of tropical Pacific islands. Eventually the archipelago collided with the North American continent and began to lift the region, while the Snake River carved ever deeper.

After taking in the views at the lookout, either drive or walk to the trailhead down the 1¼-mile rough dirt road located just to the right as you exit the lookout parking area. A large dirt parking area is located just to the right of the trailhead. If you are planning a hike in the winter or spring months, it is recommended that you walk in, since the road can become very muddy. Walk past the gate and follow the old service road through the small grove of ponderosa pine. After ½ mile

you come to another gate; pass through it and ignore the trail to the left, which leads to an old cabin. From here the views of the canyon really begin to open up. In the spring the grasslands of the canyon are filled with the yellows, reds, and lavenders of balsamroot, paintbrush, and penstemon.

As you continue down the trail another mile, stay to the left at the next junction with the very steep and difficult Tulley Creek Trail. Continuing down the exposed ridge another ½ mile brings you to Spain Saddle and another fence crossing. From here it's another ½ mile to the next and last gate. After you pass over the gate, veer to the left and follow a faint trail a few hundred feet to catch your first glimpse of the Snake River, still a distant 3,000 feet below.

Back on the main trail, another mile brings you to Eureka Point. Another faint trail to the left leads to a rocky outcrop with views of what seem to be the endless ridges of the Imnaha River Canyons and down to the Snake River and Eureka Bar.

In 1899 local miners claimed to have found copper ore in a ruse to sell shares of stock to Eastern investors. When the investors began to grow wary, the would-be miners claimed that the ore contained gold. Investors, blinded with gold fever, financed a mining expedition complete with a 120-foot-long sternwheeler capable of navigating the untamed waters of the Snake River. Almost overnight a town of 2,000 residents sprang up as a result of the arrival of the sternwheeler, which was heavily loaded with equipment needed to process the ore. However, on the day the boat was due to deliver its load, it lost control in the rapids, slammed against the canyon walls, and sank, bringing down with it the fortunes and futures of the town of Eureka. While contemplating the fate of the boomtown of

Eureka, rest here and have lunch before making the steep trip back to the trailhead.

From here the trail continues another 4 miles and drops another 2,500 feet before it reaches the Snake River at the Eureka Mine. However, it is not recommended unless you are well prepared, have plenty of water, and are in top physical condition. From the Snake River, the return hike to the trailhead is more of a test of will than an enjoyable hike.

The Hells Canyon region contains the most diverse population of wildlife in the Pacific Northwest and includes grouse, pheasant, quail, elk, mule deer, bighorn sheep, black bear, wolverine, mountain lion, coyote, and bobcat. In addition, stray wolves from Idaho have also recently been seen in the area. According to biologists it is just a matter of time before their haunting howls will once again be heard echoing in the canyon.

42

Leslie Gulch

Location: Leslie Gulch Area of Critical Environmental Concern, 43 miles north of Jordan Valley

Distance (combined round-trip): 3½ miles

Time (combined round-trip): 4 hours

Vertical rise (combined): 600 feet

Difficulty: easy

Map: USGS 7½' Rooster Comb

Best season: spring, fall

Hidden away in one of Oregon's more remote and desolate locations, Leslie Gulch offers hikers a unique and stunningly beautiful landscape. These three short hikes explore the surprising array of wildlife and plant life living in the gulch and offer a glimpse into Oregon's volatile geologic past.

Getting There

From Jordan Valley follow US 95 north 27 miles to the SUCCOR CREEK STATE RECREATION AREA sign and turn left. Follow the well-maintained gravel road 8½ miles and turn left at the junction following the LESLIE GULCH sign. Travel another 10 miles to the entrance of Leslie Gulch.

From Ontario travel east on I-84 into Idaho and the exit for US 95 (Nyssa). Follow US 95 to the SUCCOR CREEK STATE RECREATION AREA sign and turn right and follow the well-maintained gravel road another 8½ miles to the junction. Turn right, following the LESLIE GULCH sign, and travel another 10 miles to the entrance of Leslie Gulch.

Special Notes

The temperature during the summer months can easily reach above 100 degrees, so bring plenty of water and dress appropriately.

Although somewhat rare, rattlesnakes do inhabit the area. Care should be taken when stepping over or reaching into rocks or hidden areas.

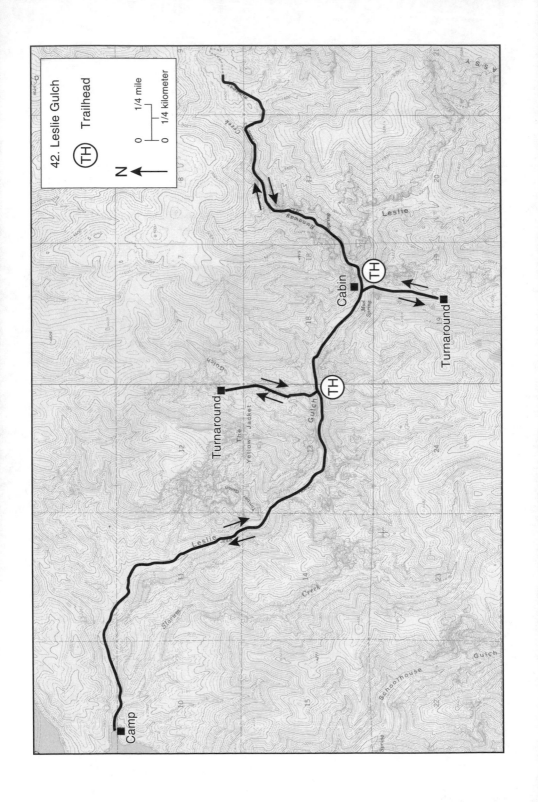

Camp

Turnaround

The Yellow Jacket

Gulch

Turnaround

(TH)

(TH)

Cabin

Leslie

Leslie   Creek

Schoolhouse

Gulch

Leslie Gulch rhyolite formation

The Trail

The Owyhee landscape is dominated by the geological events surrounding the vast network of calderas of the region. Leslie Gulch is only one product of a series of eruptions of this network beginning around 15½ million years ago and ending approximately 15 million years ago. As you pass through the gulch, you will notice an amazing variety of colors within the formation. The yellowish rock is composed of ash from the numerous flows that covered the region. The dark red rock is rhyolite, which was created when the molten lava pushed its way through the ash layers and erupted on the surface.

The first trail used to explore the area is the Dago Gulch Trail. The trailhead for Dago Gulch lies approximately 7 miles from the entrance, just opposite the small cabin at Mudd Springs. Drive a few hundred yards to the turnaround just before the locked gate and park your car. From here the trail follows the mostly level service road, through sagebrush and juniper trees, up the gulch for ¾ mile to a second gate. Turn around here since the trail beyond the gate crosses private land. Along the trail you pass the honeycombed yellow tuff cliffs composed of 15-million-year-old ash deposits and red rhyolite dikes.

Located 1 mile past Dago Gulch is the second hike through Juniper Gulch. From Dago Gulch drive or walk 1 mile west to the single-car pullout on the right near the sign marking the trailhead. From here the trail works its way through sagebrush and crosses the usually dry streambed of Leslie Creek. The trail then begins to climb up the narrow, dusty, dry wash and into the canyon. The tall vertical cliffs of tuff and rhyolite never fail to impress by either their sheer size or their intricate shapes. After ¾ mile the trail fades to an end. Although many hikers venture beyond this point, it is not recommended due to the very steep slopes and poor footing.

Continuing down the road another 3½ miles past Juniper Gulch, you arrive at the desolate Slocum campground. From here a faint trail leads up the north side of the gulch, through thick sagebrush and beneath towering orange bluffs of ash tuff, for a ½ mile before fading.

Unique photographic opportunities abound and include the numerous wildflowers, wildlife, and the walls of the gulch itself. The best light can be found right at sunrise and sunset when the soft red-and-orange light accentuates the colors of the rock.

Although it may appear to be a desolate place, Leslie Gulch is surprisingly rich in plants and wildlife. In addition to sage, balsamroot, and lupine, the gulch is also home to Packard's blazing star and Etter's groundsel, both of which are only found here. In 1965, 17 bighorn sheep were reintroduced into Leslie Gulch. Since then the herd has grown to more than 200. The best time to catch a glimpse of the sheep is in the early spring and fall. Rocky Mountain elk, mule deer, and coyotes can also be seen along with chukars, quail, hawks, eagles, swifts, and the occasional rattlesnake.

43

Jordan Craters

Location: 43 miles northwest of Jordan Valley

Distance (round-trip): 1 mile

Time (round-trip): 1 hour

Vertical rise: 150 feet

Difficulty: easy

Map: USGS 7½' Jordan Craters North

Best season: spring, fall

Looking somewhat out of place in this remote sage desert lies a maze of rock channels, lava tubes, and splatter cones, evidence of some of Oregon's most recent volcanic activity.

Getting There

From Jordan Valley follow US 95 north 8 miles to the JORDAN CRATERS sign and turn left. Follow the well-maintained gravel road 11½ miles and turn right at the junction following the JORDAN CRATERS sign. Another 6¾ miles brings you to another junction. Stay left and follow the dirt road 1½ miles to the parking area. The last mile of the road is rough and only recommended for four-wheel drive vehicles.

Special Notes

The temperature during the summer months can easily reach above 100 degrees, so bring plenty of water and plan to hike early in the morning.

Although somewhat rare, rattlesnakes do inhabit the area surrounding the lava fields. Care should be taken when stepping over rocks or hidden areas.

The Trail

Take an early morning drive to the trailhead and you are almost certain to spot a coyote hunting or mule deer and antelope grazing among the sagebrush. Early mornings and late evenings are also times to watch for snakes warming themselves on the road.

The trailhead is located just to the left of the information board located at the large

Jordan Craters lava field

gravel parking area. The trail begins by climbing up and around Coffee Pot Crater, a large, glassy, black-basalt cinder cone. From the parking area, the Coffee Pot cinder cone is moderately impressive. However, as you near the top of the trail, which brings you to a cliff-edge view of the massive crater, you begin to realize the magnitude of the events that occurred here a little more than 4,000 years ago. From here you can look southwest, over the crater toward Cow Lakes, and follow the path the lava took as it covered approximately 28 square miles of the surrounding landscape.

Continuing along the trail to the other side of the crater, you will encounter strange rock formations and several rock channels created when the still-fluid lava melted a path through the cooler lava that had already solidified. One such channel carves its way several hundred feet before diving under, creating a lava tube. If you are so inclined, a short, poorly defined trail spur to the left leads to the bottom of the crater. Use extreme caution when approaching the edge. The cliffs are unstable and the loose cinders make for slippery footing.

During the spring and summer, hundreds of cliff swallows chase insects within the crater. Hawks can be seen flying overhead looking for snakes, prairie dogs, and jackrabbits living in the sage surrounding the lava field. Marmots can also be seen scurrying from hole to hole in the lava beds.

From here, the trail continues around the rim for another ¼ mile and back to the parking area. If you want to explore the lava fields further, follow the faint trail that begins just left of the trailhead and leads ¼ mile to the string of oddly shaped splatter cones in the distance.

Jordan Craters is a result of the continental forces that have helped create and shape the Oregon landscape for millions of years. As the North American plate rode up and over the Pacific plate, the two plates stretched the state from north to south, creating cracks in the surface and allowing lava to reach the surface. These same continental forces are also responsible for Fort Rock, the Newberry Volcano, and Diamond Craters. This system is less than 4,000 years old—a reminder that this land is still active and growing.

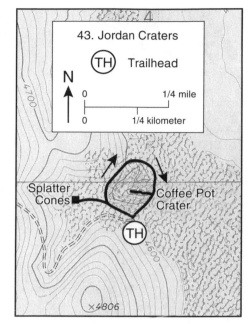

44

Oregon Trail Interpretive Center

Location: 5 miles east of Baker City

Distance (round-trip): 3 miles

Time (round-trip): 1½ hours

Vertical Gain: 350 feet

Difficulty: easy

Maps: USGS 7½' Flag Staff Hill; museum brochure

Best season: spring, summer, fall, winter

The National Oregon Trail Interpretive Center is located outside historic Baker City and perched atop Flagstaff Hill. Although the trail is short and mostly paved, it is a must-stop for visitors to eastern Oregon and those interested in the history and culture of the Northwest pioneers.

Getting There

From Baker City follow I-84 north to exit 302. Turn east onto US 86 and follow it 5 miles to the National Oregon Trail Interpretive Center entrance on the left.

Special Notes

During the summer months, it is best to hike the trail during the morning and tour the center's exhibits afterward to avoid the heat of the sun. A $10 admission fee per car is collected at the entrance booth.

The Trail

The Oregon Trail began as an unconnected series of pathways used by Native Americans. By the time the railroads made the trail obsolete in 1884, it had extended the borders of the United States from the Atlantic to the Pacific, doubling the size of the nation.

Between the years of 1843 and 1866, it is estimated that close to 500,000 pioneers left their former lives behind to brave the heat and dust of the plains and the cold and snow of precarious mountain passes to start a new life in a place they had never seen. From Independence, Missouri, they

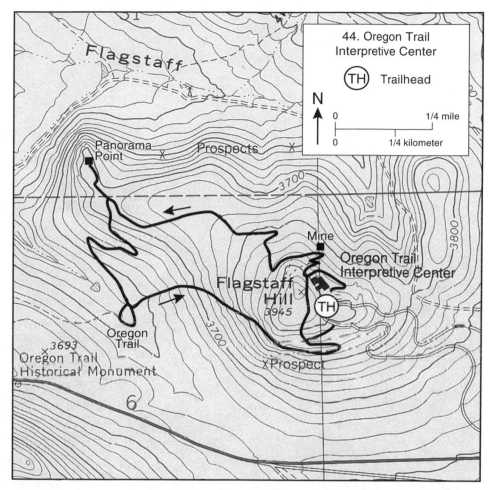

traveled nearly 2,000 miles. Some took the journey looking for adventure or seeking unknown opportunities. Others were fleeing persecution or economic strife, while still others were drawn by the promise of free land. The Oregon Donation Land Act offered up to 640 acres of free land per homestead.

For those pioneers passing this point, emotions must have surely been mixed. They had completed 80 percent of their journey and reached the Oregon Territory. However, ahead could be seen the decep-

tively rugged Blue Mountains and beyond them the Cascades with the snows of fall and winter closing in.

Beginning at the Interpretive Center, the mostly paved trail heads down the hill to a replica of a hard-rock gold mine. Such mines were once relatively common in the area. From the mine, follow the signs down 1 mile toward Panorama Point. Follow the short trail spur to the right, which leads a few hundred yards to a viewing platform and shaded bench perched just back from the cliff. The view extends beyond the path the trail once

---

Looking west on the Oregon Trail

took to the Blue Mountains in the distance. Returning back to the main trail and following it down the hill for ½ mile brings you to a four-way trail intersection. Turn right and follow the path a few hundred feet to the markers identifying the Old Oregon Trail.

Time and the elements have taken their toll on the old trail. Looking west it's possible to make out its faint outline, distinguished by the absence of wheel ruts. Unlike dirt roads created by cars, which have two distinct parallel tire ruts, trails made by animal-drawn carts make one wide rut since the hooves of the animals wear down the center.

The trail continues on for another ¼ mile, completing a small loop, passing a covered wagon replica, and then rejoining the trail at the intersection. From here you can either continue back up the same paved path you came in on, or turn right and follow the dusty, unpaved trail 1 mile up the hill back to the Interpretive Center parking area.

45

John Day Fossil Beds

Location: 10 miles northwest of Mitchell, 50 miles northeast of Prineville

Distance (combined): 3 miles

Time (combined): 3½ hours

Vertical Gain: 400 feet

Difficulty: easy

Maps: USGS 7½' Painted Hill; National Monument Trail Guide

Best season: spring, summer, fall, winter

Aside from Crater Lake and Mount Hood, the Painted Hills of the John Day Fossil Beds National Monument are one of the signature geological formations of Oregon. The vivid colors of the formation are created by layers of minerals from volcanic ash deposits dating back 30 million years. The volcanic ash has been compressed and weathered to create the colorful landscape you see today.

Getting There

From Prineville travel east 50 miles on US 26. At the sign for the John Day Fossil Beds National Monument turn left onto Bridge Creek Road (4 miles west of Mitchell). Follow Bridge Creek Road 6 miles to Bear Creek Road and turn left into the National Monument. All the trails begin on or near Bear Creek Road, which runs through the monument.

Special Notes

The colors are most vivid in the morning and evening light, especially after a good rainfall. The delicate clay that makes up the colorful formations is soft and very easily damaged, so visitors are required to stay on the designated trails to avoid destruction that heavy traffic would bring. A Northwest Forest Pass is required to park at the trailhead and is available from many private vendors ($5 daily, $30 annually).

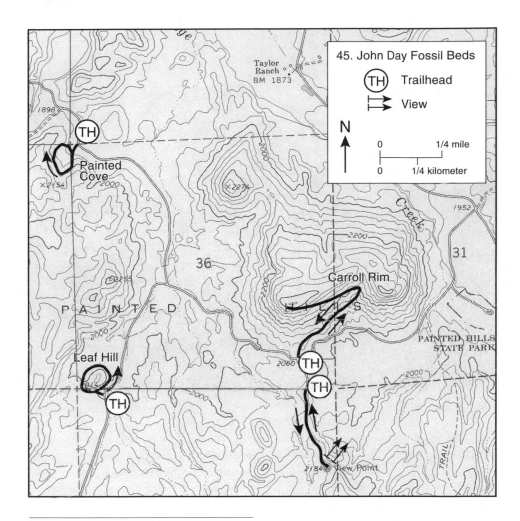

The Trail

The John Day Fossil Beds National Monument is composed of three units: the Clarno Unit, Sheep Rock Unit, and the Painted Hills Unit. While each is unique and well worth visiting, the Painted Hills Unit is the most visually unique.

Excavation of the John Day site began in the 1860s with the work of Thomas Condon, a frontier minister. By the turn of the twentieth century, researchers from the Smithsonian Institution and around the country began requesting specimens.

Researchers still painstakingly work the site, delivering thousands of specimens to the National Park Service each year. However, even with all this activity, it was not until 1975 that Congress declared the site a National Monument.

Four short trails explore the various areas of the Painted Hills. To reach the trailhead of the first trail, drive ½ mile on the monument road to the Carroll Rim trailhead marker located just opposite the road leading to the Painted Hills Overlook. From the road the trail

Painted Cove Trail

begins by climbing steeply up to the rim for ½ mile. Along the way you will enjoy a great view of the colorful Painted Hills valley below. The rim, is composed of volcanic tuff (compressed volcanic ash), which was deposited over 28 million years ago. After reaching the rim, the trail levels off and makes a sharp left to double back and follow the rim for another ½ mile through sagebrush and balsamroot, to a cliff-edge viewpoint. From the viewpoint you can look east over to Sutton Mountain, as well as survey the monument's colorful hills.

The second trail lets you enjoy a closer view of the colorful formations. To reach the trailhead, drive another 1¼ miles to the Painted Cove Trail. This short ¼-mile loop begins at the parking area and takes you around, over, and through a small formation

for a close-up view of the claylike surface of the hills. The portion of the trail that crosses over the formation is an elevated boardwalk constructed to avoid damage to the formation.

The vibrant colors are a result of the predominate minerals contained within each layer. The rust-colored layers are just that, layers rich with iron oxide. The yellow layers are a result of iron and magnesium oxides, and the black marks are manganese oxide.

The Leaf Hill Trail explores a less-colorful portion of the monument. This ¼-mile loop begins at the parking area and circles a small hill rich in plant fossils. As you continue around the far side of the hill, you come across a section of the trail that is littered with shells, all fossils from a much different landscape than what we see today. Much of what we now know of the ancient forests and vegetation of eastern Oregon has been, and still is being, learned from this site.

The fourth trail leaves you with a lasting view of the most colorful hills in the monument. The trail begins at the overlook parking lot and climbs a little more than ¼ mile along the ridgeline above the colorful rolling hills. The viewpoint at the end of the trail is perched just above the vegetation line and looks down the length of the small valley.

After hiking the monument's trails, the information and picnic area located next to Bridge Creek is a great place to have lunch and ponder the monument's geology, history, and sights. And on a final note, only a few miles upstream in Bridge Creek, a very well preserved woolly mammoth tusk was found in the streambed.

John Day Fossil Beds

46

Smith Rock

Location: Smith Rock State Park, 6 miles north of Redmond, 20 miles south of Madras

Distance (round-trip): 6 miles, Misery Ridge 4 miles

Time (round-trip): 3½ hours, 2½ hours

Vertical Gain: 200 feet, 700 feet

Difficulty: easy, moderate

Maps: USGS 7½' Redmond; Smith Rock State Park brochure

Best season: spring, fall, winter

Conspicuously jutting out of the surrounding sagebrush and farm fields, Smith Rock is a climber's paradise. This 17-million-year-old volcanic remnant draws rock climbers from throughout the Northwest and the world.

Getting There
From Madras travel south 20 miles on US 97 to Terrebonne. Turn left onto B Street and follow the park signs for another 3¼ miles to the parking area. Traveling from Redmond follow US 97 north 6 miles to Terrebonne. Turn right onto B Street and follow the SMITH ROCK STATE PARK signs.

Special Notes
This popular park is best hiked in the early morning before the numerous climbers and hikers disturb the surprisingly abundant wildlife. A $3 day-use fee is required and is available at automated machines located in the parking area.

The Trail
It is believed that Smith Rock is named after early pioneer and Linn County sheriff John Smith who came across the formation while serving as an agent for the Warm Springs Indian Agency in 1867. However, others believe that it is named for a soldier who fell to his death while camping here with his company in the early 1860s.

The colorful cliffs of the Smith Rock formation are composed of welded tuff and rhyolite, providing evidence that this was once a major center of volcanic activity dating back

High Desert

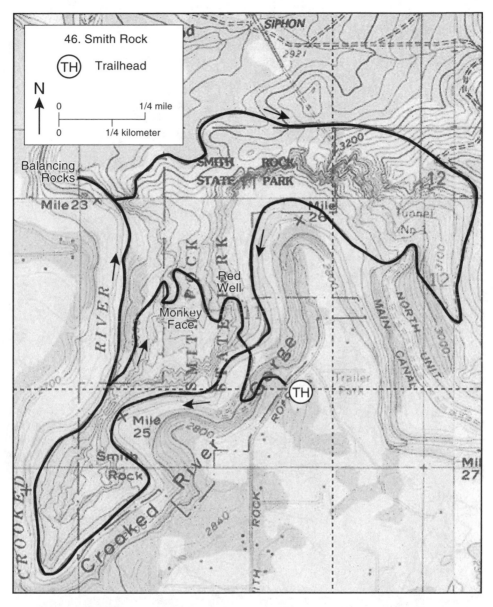

14 million years. Welded tuff and rhyolite are created under conditions of extreme heat and pressure deep in the heart of volcanic vents. Opposite Smith Rock are the dark-rimmed cliffs of basalt lava. These basalt lava flows originated from Newberry Crater located 45 miles to the south. Over 1 million years ago, these basalt flows displaced the Crooked River and forced it to carve the new canyon you see today.

Smith Rock State Park offers several hiking options, from an easy walk along the Crooked River and below the colorful cliffs to a moderately strenuous climb over the

Smith Rock over Crooked River

formation along Misery Ridge. The trail system is composed of one large loop around the rock formation, which is bisected by the Misery Ridge Trail. Several trail spurs originate off the main loop and the Misery Ridge Trail.

To reach the trail loop, walk to the overlook from the parking area and follow the steep trail down the basalt cliff. This part of the trail can be slippery in frosty or icy conditions, so care should be taken.

The loop begins at the four-way junction just across the bridge crossing the Crooked River. The right fork is the return route for the 6-mile loop, and the middle fork crosses over Smith Rock via Misery Ridge. Turn left and follow the trail along the river and around the bend beneath the towering red rhyolite dike where after ½ mile you come to Morning Glory Wall; the most popular climbing area in the park. From here several short trails lead to the rock face where numerous climbing routes begin.

Continuing along the main trail, keep an eye out for herons, eagles, and kingfishers, which frequent this area of the park. As you pass below the tuff rock formation known as the Christian Brothers, you will hear the cooing of pigeons, which echoes down the canyon. After another 1¼ miles you come to Asterisk Pass and your first views of Monkey Face, an aptly named 300-foot-high rock spire. Here, amid the juniper and sagebrush, you're likely to see deer, quail, pheasant, magpie, and perhaps a stray coyote. This is also where the trail forks; the right fork leads to the base of Monkey Face, over Misery Ridge, and back down to the bridge crossing the river.

Follow the left fork along the river for another ½ mile where you arrive at a junction. The left trail leads another ¼ mile to the balancing rocks. Here, large boulders cap ash pillars. Backtrack your way to the junction and follow the primitive trail as it ascends a steep gully through sagebrush and juniper to the top of the ridge. From here the trail levels off and follows the ridge for 1½ miles and offers views of Mount Jefferson, Mount Washington, The Three Sisters, and Black Butte as well as back over Smith Rock and the Crooked River below.

After 1½ miles, the trail meets the Burma Road; turn right and follow the very lightly used service path ¾ mile to where it meets the irrigation canal. On the right, a steep path leads past the trail register. From here the trail rejoins the river and follows it 1 mile, back to the bridge.

The Misery Ridge Trail offers a shorter but more strenuous alternative to the larger loop. From the bridge the trail climbs steeply for ¼ mile up Misery Ridge and past the Red Wall, using a series of switchbacks and staircases. Another ¼ mile brings you to the other side of the ridge and eye-level views of Monkey Face with the Cascade peaks of Mount Hood, Mount Jefferson, the Three Sisters, and Mount Washington in the distance. From here the trail leads steeply down to the base of Monkey Face and back to the main trail at Asterisk Pass after ¾ mile.

47

Fort Rock

Location: Fort Rock State Park, 68 miles southeast of Bend, Ft. Rock Valley

Distance (round-trip): 1¾ miles

Time (round-trip): 1½ hours

Vertical gain: 200 feet

Difficulty: easy

Map: USGS 7½' Fort Rock, Cabin Lake

Best season: spring, fall

Fort Rock is one of the more unique features of Oregon geology. Jutting several hundred feet out of the surrounding sagebrush desert, this ancient island was created between 50,000 and 100,000 years ago in a series of underwater eruptions in a shallow Ice Age lake.

Getting There

From Bend travel south on US 97 for 30 miles to the intersection of Highway 31, located 1½ miles south of LaPine. Turn left on Highway 31 and follow it 29 miles to County Road 5-12C (Cabin Lake Road). Turn left onto Cabin Lake Road and follow it 6 miles to the town of Fort Rock. Just past the Homestead Village Museum follow the FT. ROCK STATE PARK signs on the left for 1½ miles.

Special Notes

With an elevation of 4,400 feet, Fort Rock is part of Oregon's high desert landscape. Summer temperature extremes have been known to go from freezing at night to the 90s in the afternoon. Although rare, rattlesnakes do inhabit the area. Care should be taken when stepping over rocks or hidden areas.

The Trail

Fort Rock, geologically described as a tuft ring, was originally a full circle. Waves driven by the prevailing southeast winds gradually wore away the wall and created the horseshoe shape seen today.

The trailhead is located at the north end of the picnic parking area where a short paved path begins this easy hike into one of Oregon's many geologic wonders. The path quickly gives way to a well-defined gravel path, which leads to the east cliff viewpoint. From this viewpoint you can look along the outside of the rock's wall to the see the smooth notch carved into the cliff walls by the waves of the large Ice Age lake that once filled the valley. The waters of the lake, which covered 585 square miles and reached a maximum depth of 250 feet, slowly receded approximately 13,000 years ago. The water is now 50 feet below the ground and is the source of the aquifer that provides water the for the area's hay and alfalfa crops.

From here the trail leads to the right and enters the rock through the collapsed portion of the wall. The trail then follows an abandoned road, which, in turn, follows the

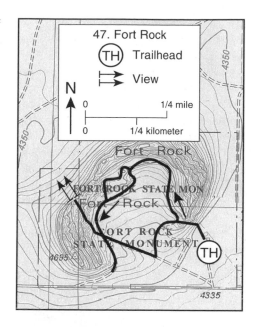

Fort Rock sunrise

cliff walls inside the ancient crater. After continuing around the loop inside the crater for a ½ mile, the trail splits into three trails. The right trail climbs up the wall of the rock to a notch in the cliff. From here you can look across the sagebrush to another much smaller tuft ring ½ mile away that is home to the Fort Rock Cave.

This cave is the source of some of the oldest human artifacts found in North America. In 1938 University of Oregon anthropologist Luther Cressman uncovered 75 sagebrush sandals along with various hunting artifacts. Radiocarbon dating of the sandals have determined the age at more than 10,000 years.

The center trail leads to the south end of the collapsed portion of the wall where evidence of the lake can again be seen in the cliff walls. The left trail follows the road back to the trailhead and parking lot ½ mile away.

The steep rock walls of Fort Rock offer protection and provide excellent habitat for raptors. Golden eagles, red-tailed hawks, and prairie falcons all inhabit the area. Cliff swallows and rock doves may also be seen. An early morning or late evening hike may yield a jackrabbit-hunting coyote or prairie dog. In addition to the endless stretches of sagebrush, early summer brings splashes of red from Indian paintbrush and yellow from balsamroot.

48

Newberry Volcano

Location: Newberry National Volcanic Monument

Distance (round-trip): ¾–8½ miles

Time (round-trip): 1–6 hours

Vertical gain: 200–500 feet

Difficulty: easy–moderate

Maps: USGS 7½' Paulina Peak, East Lake; National Monument brochure

Best season: spring, summer, fall

Paulina Lake and East Lake contained within the caldera were formed by a process similar to that which formed Crater Lake, Oregon's most famous landmark and only national park. The Newberry National Volcanic Monument offers several short hikes that will satisfy the geologist and the naturalist, as well as the family looking for a weekend getaway.

Getting There

From Bend follow US 97 south 22 miles to Forest Service Road 21, just 7 miles north of LaPine. Follow the NEWBERRY NATIONAL VOLCANIC MONUMENT sign and turn left following Forest Service Road 21 approximately 12 miles to the entrance of the National Monument.

Special Notes

As obsidian is essentially natural glass, use caution when any of the trails where it is present; a tough pair of leather boots is recommended. A Northwest Forest Pass is required to park at the trailhead and is available at the Paulina Lodge and from many private vendors ($5 daily, $30 annually).

The Trail

The Newberry National Volcanic Monument was created in 1990 and offers a unique opportunity to view one of Oregon's youngest still-active volcanic regions. While it is only a stone's throw away from the Cascades, the Newberry Volcano is actually not a Cascades volcano, but rather a member of Oregon's high lava plains, which

---

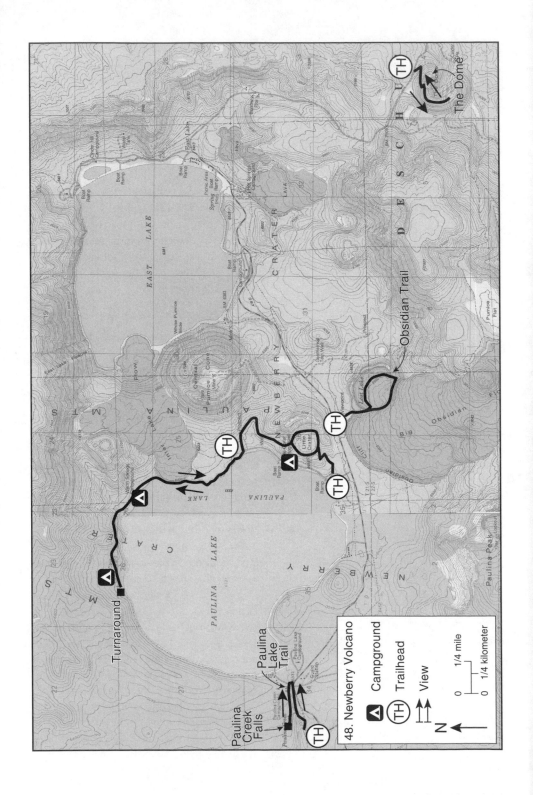

The Dome

Obsidian Trail

Turnaround

Paulina Creek Falls

Paulina Lake Trail

48. Newberry Volcano

Campground

Trailhead

View

0   1/4 mile
0   1/4 kilometer

N

Paulina Peak over Paulina Lake

encompass much of the southeastern part of the state.

Paulina Creek Falls and picnic area greet you on the left as you enter the National Monument. This short 1½-mile hike offers several views of twin 60-foot waterfalls as Paulina Creek carves through the caldera wall on its journey to the Little Deschutes River.

The trail begins at the north end of the parking area. From the parking area turn left and follow the wooded path down ¼ mile to a small rock platform and a great view from below the falls. From here, retrace your steps to the picnic area and follow the paved path to a railed viewpoint on the rim where you can watch the water tumble by onto the rocks below.

To continue on to the third viewpoint, which lies across the creek on the other side of the rim, follow the trail upstream past the picnic area where the pavement soon gives way to dirt. The trail follows the creek through a combination of fir, lodgepole, and ponderosa pine for ¼ mile to where it joins

the resort road. Cross the bridge and turn right, following the service road along the creek. After ¼ mile you'll come to a railed viewpoint along the rim looking back at the falls. To return to the trailhead, just retrace your steps.

A classic shield volcano, Newberry first erupted a little more than 1 million years ago. Approximately 500,000 years ago, major eruptions exhausted the magma beneath the volcano, and in a process similar to what occurred at Crater Lake, the 10,000-foot volcano collapsed in on itself. Rain and snow filled the newly formed caldera to create a single lake until the eruption of the central pumice cone split the lake in two 7,000 years ago. Paulina Lake takes its name from Chief Paulina of the Snake River Indians.

The 8½-mile Paulina Lake Trail begins across from the swimming area at the Little Crater Campground located just off the main road, 1½ miles past the entrance booth. From the campground, the trail immediately begins a moderate climb up the

300-foot Little Crater cinder cone. At the junction, stay to the right and follow the crater around to the viewpoint overlooking Paulina Lake, East Lake, and the central pumice cone, which helped create the two lakes. Continuing along the trail, turn right and follow the trail down to the far end of the Little Crater Campground. At this point, if you would like to return to your car, just follow the campground road back to the swimming area; otherwise turn right and continue along the lakeshore.

From the campground, the trail follows the rock-lined lakeshore for ¾ mile to the Inter-Lake Obsidian Flow. The obsidian flow occurred 7,000 years ago during the Inter-Lake Eruptive period, which also created Little Crater and the central pumice cone. Here the rocks are composed of a glassy rhyolite with heavy obsidian banding.

Following the trail another ¼ mile brings you to the Warm Springs Campground. Just offshore are submerged hot springs, an indicator that the area is still geothermally active. The springs harbor abundant algae growth and give off a smell of sulphur. Continuing on for another ¾ mile you climb to a viewpoint with another panoramic view of the caldera with the lake in the foreground and Paulina Peak looming above. The North Cove Campground, with picnic tables, a pit toilet, and a nice pebble beach, lies ½ mile ahead and makes for a nice place to turn around and complete a pleasant hike. Both the Warm Springs and North Cove campgrounds are primitive and accessible only on foot or by boat. From here, the trail follows the shoreline for another 1¾ miles until you reach the parking area of the lodge. From the lodge, the trail continues along the shore for another 2½ miles back to the Little Crater swimming area and the trailhead, should you wish to complete the lake loop.

Located ¼ mile down the main road from Little Crater is the parking area for the ¾-mile-long Obsidian Trail. You begin by walking a few hundred yards through a sparse grove of lodgepole pine where you come to a 50-foot steel staircase, which climbs the side of the obsidian flow. Dated at 1,300 years, this is the youngest lava flow in the state. The trail continues on a ½-mile loop with benches and interpretive signs, a short spur leading to a viewpoint overlooking the flow, Paulina Peak, and the cascades in the distance.

Obsidian is formed when superheated, silica-rich rhyolite cools too quickly for crystals to form. The color varies widely from black to gray depending on the amount of moisture present during the eruption. The characteristic black color is due to trace amounts of iron oxide, while the gray is a result of tiny bubbles formed when the moisture turned to steam.

The Newberry National Volcanic Monument contains more than 400 cinder cones. One of the larger ones is simply named The Dome. It can be reached by following the main road 7 miles past East Lake. The road turns to gravel approximately 2 miles before the well-marked pull-off for The Dome trailhead, located on the right.

The 1½-mile-long trail immediately begins a steep ¼-mile climb through a series of short switchbacks up the east face of the dome. As the trail levels off, the U-shaped crater becomes apparent. The shape is a result of the basalt lava flows breaching the dome walls near the end of the dome's active life. As you continue around the crater, you will be treated to yet another panoramic view of the caldera. The view to the southeast extends over the Fort Rock Valley and several dozen additional cinder cones spawned by the Newberry Volcano.

49

Big Indian Gorge

Location: Steens Mountain Wilderness Area

Distance (round-trip): 12½ miles

Time (round-trip): 8 hours

Vertical rise: 1,300 feet

Difficulty: difficult

Map: USGS 7½' Fish Lake

Best season: spring, summer, fall

Located on the western flank of Steens Mountain, Big Indian Gorge is one of the major U-shaped, glaciated canyons of the Steens Mountain Wilderness Area. A well-developed campground at the mouth of the gorge allows you to either explore the area with day excursions into the gorge and surrounding area or use it as a starting point for an overnight backpacking trip in the heart of the gorge.

Getting There

From Burns, travel southeast on US 78 1¾ miles to OR 205 and turn right following the signs to Frenchglen. Travel south on OR 205 for 71 miles, through Frenchglen, to the well-maintained and graveled Steens Mountain Loop Road. Turn left onto Steens Mountain Loop Road and follow it 20 miles to South Steens Campground. The trailhead is located just beyond the group camping area.

Special Notes

During the winter months, the trail is often covered in snow, and it can be bitter cold. In summer months, temperatures can easily reach above 100 degrees. Bring plenty of water and dress appropriately. Rattlesnakes do inhabit the area. Care should be taken when stepping over rocks or hidden areas.

Make sure you start from Burns on a full tank of gas. The closest reliable gas stations are located 100 miles away in Burns, the town of Jordan Valley, and just north of Winnemucca.

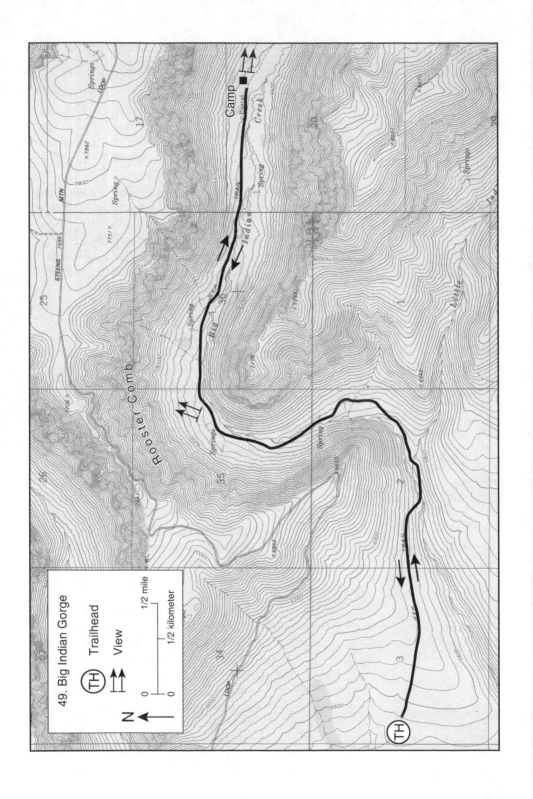

49. Big Indian Gorge

TH Trailhead

View

N

0   1/2 mile

0   1/2 kilometer

Camp

Big Indian Gorge from the Rooster Comb

The Trail

Steens Mountain is a fault-block mountain, created from a large shield volcano that began erupting 16 million years ago. (Fault-block mountains are created by the upward lift along a fault line.) Around 10 million years ago, continental forces began to lift the region more than 7,000 feet over a period of 9 million years, or a little less than 1 inch every 100 years. During the last Ice Age, Steens Mountain, along with the nearby Pueblo Mountains, were heavily glaciated. These glaciers slowly ground out the mountains' numerous U-shaped canyons and valleys.

The source of the Steens' original volcanic energy was what is now the Yellowstone hotspot (a hotspot is a stationary plume of magma pointed at the earth's crust). As the North American continent moved west, the volcanic activity associ-

ated with the hotspot appears to have moved east some 350 miles. Today the same volcanic source that created Steens Mountain now drives the geysers and thermal pools of Yellowstone National Park.

Steens Mountain is also home to another geologic oddity. As the iron-rich basalt cools, the iron crystals align themselves with the earth's magnetic field. During some of the Steens Mountain eruptions, the earth's magnetic field was in the process of reversing polarity, the North Pole becoming the South Pole. This process was thought at first to have occurred over a period of thousands of years. But, amazingly, the orientation of the iron crystals in the Steens Mountain basalt shows that the magnetic field was changing as much as 7 degrees per day, forcing geologists to rethink the mechanism of and timeframe for pole reversal.

The trailhead is at the far left end of the group campground near the boundary gate to the wilderness area. Follow the service road through sage and juniper trees to where the road ends at Big Indian Creek. If you brought sandals, now is the time for them since you will ford three creeks in the next 1¼ miles. Wade into the creek (which never gets deeper than your knees) for another ¼ mile where you meet Little Indian Creek (your second creek crossing). Ford the shallow stream. As you continue on, you soon pass the remains of an old log cabin and homestead on your left. Along the way look for jackrabbits hiding in the sagebrush. These amazing little rodents can reach speeds of nearly 40 miles per hour. After a ½ mile, you once again arrive at Big Indian Creek, the third and final creek crossing along the trail.

For the next mile the trail passes through some fairly dense sagebrush. Long pants and a tough pair of boots are recommended. Along this section of the trail, you pass below the Rooster Comb, a narrow rock wall separating Big Indian Gorge from Little Blitzen Gorge just to the north. Follow the creek as you curve your way around to a point where you can look up the gorge to the snow-streaked cliffs of the Steens Mountain head wall. Take some time to look around and enjoy the solitude as you are nearly engulfed by the gorge and its 2,000-foot-high cliffs in one of the most remote areas of the state.

As you continue along the creek, cottonwood and aspen trees begin to outnumber the juniper. Wildflowers such as paintbrush, lupine, and penstemon add color in the spring. After following the creek for another 2½ miles, you reach a small primitive campsite in a small grassy meadow. A grove of cottonwoods growing next to the creek provides some welcome shade before setting up camp or heading back to the trailhead.

In addition to the jackrabbits, you may also encounter mule deer, porcupines, and marmots. Patrolling the skies are golden eagles, red-tailed hawks, and prairie falcons.

50

Pike Creek

Location: east side of Steens Mountain Wilderness Area

Distance (round-trip): 2¾ miles

Time (round-trip): 3 hours

Vertical Rise: 850 feet

Difficulty: easy

Map: USGS 7½' Alvord Hot Springs

Best season: spring, fall

On the east side of Steens Mountain, an old mining road offers a pleasant hike between the snowcapped peaks of Steens Mountain and sunbaked alkali flats of Alvord Desert.

Getting There

From Burns, travel southeast on US 78 for 65 miles, passing through Crane and Princeton, to East Steens Road and the sign pointing to Fields. Turn right onto the well-maintained gravel road and travel approximately 40 miles to the Alvord Ranch on the left and look for the unmarked road to the trailhead just 3½ miles past the ranch entrance. From the cattle guard to the primitive campground, it's ½ mile of rough, rutted, dirt road and only recommended for vehicles with four-wheel drive.

Special Notes

During the winter months, the trail is often covered in snow and it can be bitter cold. In summer months, temperatures can easily reach above 100 degrees. Bring plenty of water and dress appropriately. Make sure you start from Burns on a full tank of gas. The closest reliable gas stations are located 100 miles away in Burns, the town of Jordan Valley, and just north of Winnemucca.

Rattlesnakes do inhabit the area. Care should be taken when stepping over rocks or hidden areas.

The Trail

The trailhead is located just above the primitive campground on the north side of the

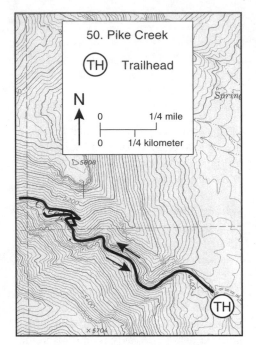

50. Pike Creek

(TH) Trailhead

N

0   1/4 mile

0   1/4 kilometer

creek. The trail begins by crossing Pike Creek near the large boulder with a large juniper tree appearing to grow out of it. The creek is shallow and can easily be forded by hopping across rocks. From here you'll join an old, abandoned mining road and follow it as it winds up the canyon along the creek. The trail passes through large and silver sagebrush, and rabbitbrush, as well as wildflowers of balsamroot, lupine, and penstemon. As you continue the moderate climb, you pass a small, picturesque rock arch on the north side of the canyon.

After a mile, you pass the remnants of an unsuccessful 1950s uranium mine with the entrance to the shaft just above the trail. Soon after, the trail passes through a small grove of cottonwood trees, which offer some shade and a welcome relief from the sun. From here the trail crosses the creek

and begins a short, steep ½ mile climb through a series of switchbacks. Near the crest of the trail, gem hunters have sorted through the rock nodules in search of thunder eggs, Oregon's state rock.

Thunder eggs are a type of geode, a shell of rock formed around a conglomerate of minerals, usually quartz or feldspar. They form in rhyolite lava beds where volcanic gases left bubbles frozen into the rock. Over time, mineral-rich solutions entered the void and created the crystalline filling. The name "Thunder Egg" is derived from a Native American legend about the spirits of Mount Hood and Mount Jefferson who robbed the "eggs" from nests of "Thunderbirds" (spirits Native Americans considered to be very powerful).

As you continue on for the last few hundred yards, ignore the trail fork to the right at the summit, which leads to Pike Knob, and continue to the end of the trail to a small shaded ledge overlooking the creek. The trail's end is a great place to have lunch before heading back down to the trailhead.

On the way back, take some time to gaze out at the white expanse of the Alvord Desert. This alkali flat, the remnant of an Ice Age lake, is ironically now the driest area in Oregon with an annual precipitation of less than 6 inches a year. You may also catch a glimpse of land sailors (similar to iceboats but with wheels) racing across the desert, taking advantage of the smooth surface and persistent wind.

Wildlife you may see along the way include coyotes, antelopes, and deer. Redtailed hawks, Swainson's hawks, ferruginous hawks, and prairie falcons can all be seen flying in search of pygmy rabbits, ground squirrels, and sage grouse.

Steens Mt. near Pike Creek

Index

Let Countryman Take You There

Our experienced backcountry authors will lead you to the finest trails, parks, and back roads in the following areas:

50 Hikes Series
Northeast
50 Hikes in Connecticut
50 Hikes in the Maine Mountains
50 Hikes in Coastal and Southern Maine
50 Hikes in Massachusetts
50 Hikes in the White Mountains
50 More Hikes in New Hampshire
50 Hikes in the Adirondacks
50 Hikes in the Lower Hudson Valley
50 Hikes in Central New York
50 Hikes in Western New York
50 Hikes in Vermont
Mid-Atlantic
50 Hikes in Maryland
50 Hikes in New Jersey
50 Hikes in Central Pennsylvania
50 Hikes in Eastern Pennsylvania
50 Hikes in Western Pennsylvania
50 Hikes in Northern Virginia
50 Hikes in Southern Virginia
Southeast
50 Hikes in West Virginia
50 Hikes in Kentucky
50 Hikes in Louisiana
50 Hikes in the Mountains of North Carolina
50 Hikes in the Tennessee Mountains
50 Hikes in Central Florida
50 Hikes in North Florida
50 Hikes in South Florida
West & Midwest
50 Hikes in Arizona
50 Hikes in Colorado
50 Hikes in Michigan
50 Hikes in Ohio
50 More Hikes in Ohio
50 Hikes in Washington
50 Hikes in Wisconsin
50 Hikes in Oregon

Hiking, Climbing, Fishing & Travel
Crossing Arizona
Arizona Trout Streams and Their Hatches
Fly-Fishing the South Atlantic Coast
Alaska on Foot
American Rock
Backwoods Ethics
The California Coast

Bicycling
Northeast
Backroad Bicycling in Connecticut
25 Bicycle Tours in Maine
25 Bicycle Tours in Vermont
Backroad Bicycling on Cape Cod, Martha's
  Vineyard, and Nantucket
25 Mountain Bike Tours in Massachusetts
Backroad Bicycling in Western Massachusetts
Bike Rides in the Berkshire Hills
Bakcroad Bicycling in New Hampshire
25 Bicycle Tours in the Adirondacks
25 Bicycle Tours in the Lake Champlain Region
25 Mountain Bike Tours in the Adirondacks
Backroad Bicycling in the Finger Lakes Region
25 Bicycle Tours in the Hudson Valley
Backroad Bicycling Near New York City
The Mountain Biker's Guide to Ski Resorts
Mid-Atlantic
25 Bicycle Tours on Delmarva
25 Bicycle Tours in Maryland
30 Bicycle Tours in New Jersey
25 Mountain Bike Tours in New Jersey
Backroad Bicycling in Eastern Pennsylvania
25 Bicycle Tours in and around Washington, D.C.
Southeast
Backroad Bicycling in the Blue Ridge and Smoky
  Mountains
Backroad Bicycling in Kentucky's Bluegrass
25 Bicycle Toursin the Savannah & the Carolina
  Low Country
West & Midwest
Bicycling America's National Parks: Arizona &
  New Mexico
Bicycling America's National Parks: California
Bicycling America's National Parks: Oregon and
  Washington
Bicycling America's National Parks: Utah and
  Colorado
25 Bicycle Tours in the Texas Hill Country and
  West Texas
Backroad Bicycling in Wisconsin
25 Bicycle Tours in the Twin Cities &
  Southeastern Minnesota
Latin America
Bicycling Cuba

. . . and more!

We offer many more books on hiking, fly-fishing, travel, nature, and other subjects. Our books are available at bookstores and outdoor stores everywhere. For more information or a free catalog, call 1-800-245-4151 or write to us at The Countryman Press, P.O. Box 748, Woodstock, Vermont 05091. You can find us on the Internet at www.countrymanpress.com.